More Stories for the HEART

Over 100 Stories to

Warm Your Heart

Compiled by Alice Gray

Multnomah Publishers, Inc.
Sisters, Oregon

This Billy Graham Evangelistic Association
special edition is published with permission
from Multnomah Publishers, Inc.

MORE STORIES FOR THE HEART
© 1997 by Multnomah Publishers, Inc.

Published by Multnomah Gift Books
a Division of Multnomah Publishers, Inc.

Grateful acknowledgment is made to the many authors and
publishers for granting permission to reprint their stories.
Please see detailed information in the note section,
beginning on page 265.

Compiled by Alice Gray
Cover photograph: David Bailey

Printed in the United States of America.

Unless otherwise indicated, scripture quotations are from *The
Holy Bible: New International Version,* © 1973, 1978, 1984 by
International Bible Society. Used by permission of Zondervan
Publishing House. All rights reserved.

Also quoted: The King James Version (KJV).

For information:
MULTNOMAH PUBLISHERS, INC.
POST OFFICE BOX 1720
SISTERS, OREGON 97759

Library of Congress Cataloging-in-Publication Data
More Stories for the Heart/compiled by Alice Gray.
    p.cm.
    ISBN 0-913367-81-8
    1. Christian life--Miscellanea. I. Gray, Alice, 1939-
BV4515.2.M665   1997   97-3234

To my friends who shared their stories—
To my husband, Al, who read them with me—

We laughed and cried together.

Without the help of friends, this would be
a book of empty pages.
I especially want to thank—

John Van Diest, Associate Publisher
who believed in the idea for both
the original *Stories for the Heart* and this second edition.

Casandra Lindell
who not only made order out of chaos
but added sparkling touches to it all.

Nancy Larson and Marilyn McAuley
who helped and encouraged and brought me chocolate.

Karen Jamison
who was my cheerleader from the beginning.

Nola Bertelson, Faye Brown, Glenda Hotton, Doris Sanford,
Joan Sparks, Verna Turner, Tress Van Diest, and others
from across the country who shared their treasured stories.

My family
who encouraged me with tender words,
understanding and random deeds of love.

Stories

*Enlarge my heart with a story
and change me by the characters I meet there.*

KEN GIRE

FROM *WINDOWS OF THE SOUL*

Contents

Compassion

COMFORTING

A little girl lost a playmate in death and one day reported to her family that she had gone to comfort the sorrowing mother. "What did you say?" asked her father. "Nothing," she replied, "I just climbed up on her lap and cried with her."

Charles Swindoll

I Want That One

Charles Stanley

I heard a story once about a farmer who had some puppies for sale. He made a sign advertising the pups and nailed it to a post on the edge of his yard. As he was nailing the sign to the post, he felt a tug on his overalls. He looked down to see a little boy with a big grin and something in his hand.

"Mister," he said, "I want to buy one of your puppies."

"Well," said the farmer, "these puppies come from fine parents and cost a good deal."

The boy dropped his head for a moment, then looked back up at the farmer and said, "I've got thirty-nine cents. Is that enough to take a look?"

"Sure," said the farmer, and with that he whistled and called out, "Dolly. Here, Dolly." Out from the doghouse and down the ramp ran Dolly followed by four little balls of fur. The little boy's eyes danced with delight.

Then out from the doghouse peeked another little ball; this one noticeably smaller. Down the ramp it slid and began hobbling in an unrewarded attempt to catch up with the others. The pup was clearly the runt of the litter.

The little boy pressed his face to the fence and cried out, "I want that one," pointing to the runt.

The farmer knelt down and said, "Son, you don't want that puppy. He will never be able to run and play with you the way you would like."

With that the boy reached down and slowly pulled up one leg of his trousers. In doing so he revealed a steel brace running down both sides of his leg attaching itself to a specially made shoe. Looking up at the farmer, he said, "You see, sir, I don't run too well myself, and he will need someone who understands."

He Needed a Son

Author Unknown

The nurse escorted a tired, anxious young man to the bedside of an elderly man. "Your son is here," she whispered to the patient. She had to repeat the words several times before the patient's eyes opened. He was heavily sedated because of the pain of his heart attack and he dimly saw the young man standing outside the oxygen tent.

He reached out his hand and the young man tightly wrapped his fingers around it, squeezing a message of encouragement. The nurse brought a chair next to the bedside. All through the night the young man sat holding the old man's hand and offering gentle words of hope. The dying man said nothing as he held tightly to his son.

As dawn approached, the patient died. The young man placed on the bed the lifeless hand he had been holding, then he went to notify the nurse. While the nurse did what was necessary, the young man waited. When she had finished her task, the nurse began to offer words of sympathy to the young man. But he interrupted her.

"Who was that man?" he asked.

The startled nurse replied, "I thought he was your father."

"No, he was not my father," he answered. "I never saw him before in my life."

"Then why didn't you say something when I took you to him?" asked the nurse.

He replied, "I also knew he needed his son, and his son just wasn't here. When I realized he was too sick to tell whether or not I was his son, I knew how much he needed me."

Significance

R. C. Sproul

I had a college student who was a victim of cerebral palsy. He was able to walk, but with great difficulty as his legs and arms would fly in all directions, out of control of the motor impulses which make walking a normally simple task. His speech was slurred, slow and agonizing, demanding great concentration on the part of the listener to understand. There was nothing wrong with his mind, however, and his sparkling personality and spontaneous smile were an inspiration to his classmates and to all who encountered him.

One day he came to me vexed by a problem and asked me to pray for him. In the course of the prayer, I said something routine, with words like, "Oh, God, please help this man as he wrestles with his problem." When I opened my eyes the student was quietly weeping.

I asked him what was wrong and he stammered his reply, "You called me a man—no one has ever called me a man before."

Information Please

Paul Villiard

When I was quite young, my family had one of the first telephones in our neighborhood. I remember well the polished oak case fastened to the wall on the lower stair landing. The shiny receiver hung on the side of the box. I even remember the number—105. I was too little to reach the telephone, but used to listen with fascination when my mother talked to it. Once she lifted me up to speak to my father, who was away on business. Magic!

Then I discovered that somewhere inside that wonderful device lived an amazing person—her name was "Information Please" and there was nothing she did not know. My mother could ask her for anybody's number; when our clock ran down, Information Please immediately supplied the right time.

My first personal experience with this genie-in-the-receiver came one day while my mother was visiting a neighbor. Amusing myself at the toolbench in the basement, I whacked my finger with a hammer. The pain was terrible, but there didn't seem to be much use crying because there was no one home to offer sympathy. I walked around the house sucking my throbbing finger, finally arriving at the stairway. The telephone! Quickly I ran for the footstool in the parlor and dragged it to the landing. Climbing up, I unhooked the receiver and held it to my ear. "Information Please," I said into the mouthpiece just above my head.

A click or two, and a small, clear voice spoke into my ear. "Information."

"I hurt my fingerrr—" I wailed into the phone. The tears came readily enough, now that I had an audience.

"Isn't your mother home?" came the question.

"Nobody's home but me," I blubbered.

"Are you bleeding?"

"No," I replied. "I hit it with the hammer and it hurts."

"Can you open your ice box?" she asked. I said I could.

"Then chip off a little piece of ice and hold it to your finger. That will stop the hurt. Be careful when you use the ice pick," she admonished. "And don't cry. You'll be all right."

After that, I called Information Please for everything. I asked for help with my geography and she told me where Philadelphia was, and the Orinoco—the romantic river I was going to explore when I grew up. She helped me with my arithmetic, and she told me that a pet chipmunk—I had caught him in the park just the day before—would eat fruit and nuts.

And there was the time that Petey, our pet canary, died. I called Information Please and told her the sad story. She listened, then said the usual things grown-ups say to soothe a child. But I was unconsoled: Why was it that birds should sing so beautifully and bring joy to whole families, only to end up as a heap of feathers feet up, on the bottom of a cage?

She must have sensed my deep concern, for she said quietly, "Paul, always remember that there are other worlds to sing in."

Somehow I felt better.

Another day I was at the telephone. "Information," said the now familiar voice.

"How do you spell fix?" I asked.

"Fix something? F-I-X."

At that instant my sister, who took unholy joy in scaring me, jumped off the stairs at me with a banshee shriek—"Yaaaaaaaaaa!" I fell off the stool, pulling the receiver out of the box by the roots. We were both terrified—Information Please was no longer there, and I was not at all sure that I hadn't hurt her when I pulled the receiver out.

Minutes later there was a man on the porch. "I'm a telephone repairman. I was working down the street and the operator said there might be some trouble at this number." He reached for the receiver in my hand. "What happened?"

I told him.

"Well, we can fix that in a minute or two." He opened the telephone box, exposing a maze of wires and coils, and fiddled for a while with the end of the receiver cord, tightening things with a small screwdriver. He jiggled the hook up and down a few times, then spoke into the phone. "Hi, this is Pete. Everything's under control at 105. The kid's sister scared him and he pulled the cord out of the box."

He hung up, smiled, gave me a pat on the head and walked out the door.

All this took place in a small town in the Pacific Northwest. Then, when I was nine years old, we moved across the country to Boston—and I missed my mentor acutely. Information Please belonged in that old wooden box back home, and I somehow never thought of trying the tall, skinny new phone that sat on a small table in the hall.

Yet as I grew into my teens, the memories of those childhood conversations never really left me; often in moments of doubt and perplexity I would recall the serene sense of security I had when I knew that I could call Information Please and get the right answer. I appreciate now how very patient, understanding and kind she was to have wasted her time on a little boy.

A few years later, on my way west to college, my plane put down in Seattle. I had about half an hour between plane connections, and I spent 15 minutes or so on the phone with my sister who lived there now, happily mellowed by marriage and motherhood. Then, really without thinking what I was doing, I dialed my hometown operator and said, "Information Please."

Miraculously, I heard again the small, clear voice I knew so well: "Information."

I hadn't planned this, but I heard myself saying, "Could you tell me, please, how to spell the word 'fix'?"

There was a long pause. Then came the softly spoken answer. "I guess," said Information Please, "that your finger must have healed by now."

I laughed. "So it's really still you. I wonder if you have any idea how much you meant to me during all that time...."

"I wonder," she replied, "if you know how much you meant to me? I never had any children, and I used to look forward to your calls. Silly, wasn't it?"

It didn't seem silly, but I didn't say so. Instead I told her how often I had thought of her over the years, and I asked if I could call her again when I came back to visit my sister after the first semester was over.

"Please do. Just ask for Sally."

"Good-bye, Sally." It sounded strange for Information Please to have a name. "If I run into any chipmunks, I'll tell them to eat fruit and nuts."

"Do that," she said. "And I expect one of these days you'll be off for the Orinoco. Well, good-bye."

Just three months later I was back again at the Seattle airport. A different voice answered, "Information," and I asked for Sally.

"Are you a friend?"

"Yes," I said. "An old friend."

"Then I'm sorry to have to tell you. Sally had only been working part-time in the last few years because she was ill. She died five weeks ago." But before I could hang up, she said, "Wait a minute. Did you say your name was Villiard?"

"Yes."

"Well, Sally left a message for you. She wrote it down."

"What was it?" I asked, almost knowing in advance what it would be.

"Here it is, I'll read it—'Tell him I still say there are other worlds to sing in. He'll know what I mean.'"

I thanked her and hung up. I did know what Sally meant.

FRAGRANCE

Happiness is a perfume you cannot pour on others without getting a few drops on yourself.

George Bernard Shaw

Beethoven's Gift

Philip Yancey

A story is told about Beethoven, a man not known for social grace. Because of his deafness, he found conversation difficult and humiliating. When he heard of the death of a friend's son, Beethoven hurried to the house, overcome with grief. He had no words of comfort to offer. But he saw a piano in the room. For the next half hour he played the piano, pouring out his emotions in the most eloquent way he could. When he finished playing, he left. The friend later remarked that no one else's visit had meant so much.

I'm not so concerned you have fallen
but that you rise.

Abraham Lincoln

At the Winter Feeder

John Leax

His feather flame doused dull
by ice and cold,
the cardinal hunched
into the rough, green feeder
but ate no seed.

Through binoculars I saw
festered and useless
his beak, broken
at the root.

Then two: one blazing, one gray,
rode the swirling weather
into my vision
and lighted at his side.

Unhurried, as if possessing
the patience of God,
they cracked sunflowers
and fed him
beak to wounded beak
choice meats.

Each morning and afternoon
the winter long,
that odd triumvirate,
that trinity of need,
returned and ate
their sacrament
of broken seed.

Lonesome

Author Unknown

1904

The boy sat huddled so close to the woman in gray that everybody felt sure he belonged to her; so when he unconsciously dug his muddy shoes into the broadcloth skirt of his left-hand neighbor she leaned over and said: "Pardon me, madam, will you kindly make your little boy square himself around? He is soiling my skirt with his muddy shoes."

The woman in gray blushed a little and nudged the boy away.

"My boy?" she said. "My goodness, he isn't mine."

The boy squirmed uneasily. He was such a little fellow that he could not touch his feet to the floor, so he stuck them out straight in front of him like pegs to hang things on, and looked at them deprecatingly.

"I am sorry I got your dress dirty," he said to the woman on his left. "I hope it will brush off."

"Oh, it doesn't matter," she said. Then, as his eyes were still fastened on hers, she added: "Are you going uptown alone?"

"Yes, ma'am," he said. "I always go alone. There isn't anybody to go with me. Father is dead and mother is dead. I live with Aunt Clara in Brooklyn, but she says Aunt Anna ought to help do something for me, so once or twice a week, when she gets tired and wants to go some place to get rested up, she sends me over to stay with Aunt Anna. I am going up there now. Sometimes I don't find Aunt Anna home, but I hope she will be at home today, because it looks as if it is going to rain, and I don't like to hang around in the street in the rain."

The woman felt something uncomfortable in her throat, and she said: "You are a very little boy to be knocked about this way," rather unsteadily.

"Oh, I don't mind," he said. "I never get lost. But I get lonesome sometimes on the long trips, and when I see anybody that I think I would like to belong to I scrooge up close to her so I can make believe that I really do belong to her. This morning I was playing that I belonged to that lady on the other side of me, and I forgot all about my feet. That is why I got your dress dirty."

The woman put her arm around the tiny chap and "scrooged" him up so close that she almost hurt him, and every other woman who had heard his artless confidence looked as if she would not only let him wipe his shoes on her best gown, but would rather he did it than not.

MIND AND HEART

"And what is as important as knowledge?"
asked the mind—
"Caring, and seeing with the heart,"
answered the soul.

Author Unknown

"Make Me Like Joe!"

Tony Campolo

Joe was a drunk who was miraculously converted at a Bowery mission. Prior to his conversion, he had gained the reputation of being a dirty wino for whom there was no hope, only a miserable existence in the ghetto. But following his conversion to a new life with God, everything changed. Joe became the most caring person that anyone associated with the mission had ever known. Joe spent his days and nights hanging out at the mission, doing whatever needed to be done. There was never anything that he was asked to do that he considered beneath him. Whether it was cleaning up the vomit left by some violently sick alcoholic or scrubbing toilets after careless men left the men's room filthy, Joe did what was asked with a smile on his face and a seeming gratitude for the chance to help. He could be counted on to feed feeble men who wandered off the street and into the mission, and to undress and tuck into bed men who were too out of it to take care of themselves.

One evening, when the director of the mission was delivering his evening evangelistic message to the usual crowd of still and sullen men with drooped heads, there was one man who looked up, came down the aisle to the altar, and knelt to pray, crying out for God to help him to change. The repentant drunk kept shouting, "Oh God! Make me like Joe! Make me like Joe! Make me like Joe! Make me like Joe!"

The director of the mission leaned over and said to the man, "Son, I think it would be better if you prayed, 'Make me like *Jesus.*'"

The man looked up at the director with a quizzical expression on his face and asked, "Is he like Joe?"

Lady, Are You Rich?

Marion Doolan

They huddled inside the storm door—two children in ragged outgrown coats.

"Any old papers, lady?"

I was busy. I wanted to say no—until I looked down at their feet. Thin little sandals, sopped with sleet. "Come in and I'll make you a cup of hot cocoa." There was no conversation. Their soggy sandals left marks upon the hearthstone.

I served them cocoa and toast with jam to fortify against the chill outside. Then I went back to the kitchen and started again on my household budget....

The silence in the front room struck through to me. I looked in.

The girl held the empty cup in her hands, looking at it. The boy asked in a flat voice, "Lady...are you rich?"

"Am I rich? Mercy, no!" I looked at my shabby slip covers.

The girl put her cup back in its saucer—carefully. "Your cups match your saucers." Her voice was old, with a hunger that was not of the stomach.

They left then, holding their bundles of papers against the wind. They hadn't said thank you. They didn't need to. They had done more than that. Plain blue pottery cups and saucers. But they matched. I tested the potatoes and stirred the gravy. Potatoes and brown gravy, a roof over our heads, my man with a good steady job—these things matched, too.

I moved the chairs back from the fire and tidied the living room. The muddy prints of small sandals were still wet upon my hearth. I let them be. I want them there in case I ever forget again how very rich I am.

To My Neighbor

Mother Teresa

O ne night a man came to our house and told me, "There is a family with eight children. They have not eaten for days." I took some food with me and went.

When I finally came to that family, I saw the faces of those little children disfigured by hunger. There was no sorrow or sadness in their faces, just the deep pain of hunger.

I gave the rice to the mother. She divided the rice in two, and went out, carrying half the rice. When she came back, I asked her, "Where did you go?" She gave me this simple answer, "To my neighbors—they are hungry also!"

...I was not surprised that she gave, because poor people are really very generous. But I was surprised that she knew they were hungry. As a rule, when we are suffering, we are so focused on ourselves we have no time for others.

Real friends are those who,
when you've made a fool of yourself,
don't feel that you've done a permanent job.

Erwin T. Randall

A Guy Named Bill

Rebecca Manley Pippert
Retold by Alice Gray

His name is Bill. He has wild hair, wears a T-shirt with holes in it, jeans and no shoes. This was literally his wardrobe for his entire four years of college.

He is brilliant. Kinda esoteric and very, very bright. He became a Christian while attending college. Across the street from the campus is a well-dressed, very conservative church. They want to develop a ministry to the students, but are not sure how to go about it.

One day Bill decides to go there. He walks in with no shoes, jeans, his T-shirt, and wild hair. The service has already started and so Bill starts down the aisle looking for a seat. The church is completely packed and he can't find a seat. By now people are looking a bit uncomfortable, but no one says anything.

Bill gets closer and closer and closer to the pulpit and when he realizes there are no seats, he just squats down right on the carpet. (Although perfectly acceptable behavior at a college fellowship, trust me, this had never happened in this church before!) By now the people are really uptight, and the tension in the air is thick.

About this time, the minister realizes that from way at the back of the church, a deacon is slowly making his way toward Bill. Now the deacon is in his eighties, has silver-gray hair, a three-piece suit, and a pocket watch. A godly man—very elegant, very dignified, very courtly. He walks with a cane and as he starts walking toward this boy, everyone is saying to themselves, *You can't blame him for what he's going to do. How can you expect a man of his age and of his background to understand some college kid on the floor?*

It takes a long time for the man to reach the boy. The church is utterly silent except for the clicking of the man's cane. All eyes are focused on him; you can't even hear anyone breathing. The people are thinking, *The minister can't even preach the sermon until the deacon does what he has to do.*

And now they see this elderly man drop his cane on the floor. With great difficulty he lowers himself and sits down next to Bill and worships with him so he won't be alone. Everyone chokes up with the emotion. When the minister gains control he says, "What I'm about to preach, you will never remember. What you have just seen, you will never forget."

Autumn Dance

Robin Jones Gunn

She stood a short distance from her guardian at the park this afternoon, her distinctive features revealing that although her body blossomed into young adulthood, her mind would always remain a child's. My children ran and jumped and sifted sand through perfect, coordinated fingers. Caught up in fighting over a shovel, they didn't notice when the wind changed. But she did. A wild autumn wind spinning leaves into amber flurries.

I called to my boisterous son and jostled my daughter. Time to go. Mom still has lots to do today. My rosy-cheeked boy stood tall, watching with wide-eyed fascination the gyrating dance of the Down's syndrome girl as she scooped up leaves and showered herself with a twirling rain of autumn jubilation.

With each twist and hop she sang deep, earthy grunts—a canticle of praise meant only for the One whose breath causes the leaves to tremble from the trees.

Hurry up. Let's go. Seat belts on? I start the car. In the rearview mirror I study her one more time through misty eyes. And then the tears come. Not tears of pity for her. The tears are for me. For I am far too sophisticated to publicly shout praises to my Creator.

I am whole and intelligent and normal, and so I weep because I will never know the severe mercy that frees such a child and bids her come dance in the autumn leaves.

To My Nurses

Author Unknown

What do you see, nurse, what do you see?
Maybe you are thinking when you look at me:
A crabbed old woman, not very wise,
Uncertain of habit with faraway eyes,
Who dribbles her food and makes no reply
When you say in a loud voice,
"I do wish you'd try"?
Who seems not to notice the things that you do
And forever is losing a stocking or shoes,
Who resisting or not, lets you do as you will
With bathing and feeding, the long day to fill.
Is that what you're thinking, is that what you see?
Then open your eyes, nurse. You're not looking at me.
I'll tell you who I am as I sit here so still.
As I move at your bidding, eat at your will,
I'm a small child of ten with father and mother,
Brothers and sisters who love one another;
A young girl of sixteen with wings on her feet,
Dreaming that soon a love she'll meet;
A bride at twenty, my heart gives a leap,
Remembering the vows that I promised to keep;
At twenty-five now I have young of my own
Who need me to build a secure, happy home.
A woman of thirty, my young now grow fast,
Bound together with ties that should last.
At forty, my young sons have grown up and gone,
But my man's beside me to see I don't mourn.
At fifty once more babies play round my knee—
Again we know children, my loved one and me.

Dark days are upon me, my husband is dead.
I look to the future, I shudder with dread.
For my young are all rearing young of their own,
And I think of the years and the love that I've known.

I'm an old woman now and nature is cruel.
It is her jest to make old age look like a fool.
The body crumbles, grace and vigor depart.
There is a stone where I once had a heart.
But inside this old carcass a young girl still dwells,
And now again my bittered heart swells.
I remember the joys, I remember the pain
And I'm loving and living life over again.
I think of the years, all too few, gone too fast,
And accept the stark fact that nothing can last.
So open your eyes, nurse, open and see
Not a crabbed old woman,
Look closer—see me!

A Second Chance

Billy Graham

Georgia Tech played the University of California in the 1929 Rose Bowl. In the game a player recovered a fumble, but became confused and ran the wrong way. A teammate tackled him just before he would have scored a touchdown against his own team. At halftime all of the players went into the dressing room and sat down, wondering what the coach would say. This young man sat by himself; put a towel over his head, and cried.

When the team was ready to go back onto the field for the second half, the coach stunned the team when he announced that the same players who had started the first half would start the second. All of the players left the dressing room except this young man. He would not budge. The coach looked back as he called him again, and saw that his cheeks were wet with tears. The player said, "Coach, I can't do it. I've ruined you. I've disgraced the University of California. I can't face that crowd in the stadium again."

Then the coach put his hand on the player's shoulder and said, "Get up and go back in. The game is only half over."

When I think of that story, deep inside I say, "What a coach!" When I read the story of Jonah [in the Bible], and the stories of thousands like him, I say, "To think that God would give me another chance!"

Eternal Harmony

John MacArthur
Retold by Casandra Lindell

C enturies ago, it was known far and wide that a certain tribal leader was the greatest in all the tribes. When power was measured by proving superior physical strength, the most powerful tribe of all was the one that had the strongest leader.

But this tribal leader was also known for his wisdom. In order to help his people live safely and peacefully, he carefully put laws into place guiding every aspect of tribal life. The leader enforced those laws strictly and had long ago acquired a reputation for uncompromising justice.

In spite of the laws, there were problems. One day it came to the leader's attention that someone in the tribe was stealing. He called the people together.

"You know that the laws are for your protection, to help you live safely and in peace," he reminded them, his eyes heavy with sadness because of his love for them. "This stealing must stop. We all have what we need. The penalty has been increased from ten to twenty lashes from the whip for the person caught stealing."

But the thief continued to take things that didn't belong to him, so the leader called all the people together again.

"Please hear me," he pled with them. "This must stop. It hurts us all and makes us feel bad about each other. The penalty has been increased to thirty lashes."

Still, the stealing continued. The leader gathered the people together once more.

"Please, I'm begging you. For *your* sake, this has to stop. The pain it is causing among us is too great. The penalty has been increased to forty lashes from the whip." The people knew of their leader's great love for them, but only those closest to him saw the single tear make its way slowly down his face as he dismissed the gathering.

Finally, a man came to say the thief had been caught. The word had spread. Everyone had gathered to see who it was.

A single gasp raced through the crowd as the thief emerged between two guards. The tribal leader's face fell in shock and grief.

The thief was his very own mother, old and frail.

What will he do? the people wondered aloud, a hushed murmur fanning out. Would he uphold the law or would his love for his mother win over it? The people waited, talking quietly collectively holding their breath.

Finally their leader spoke. "My beloved people." His voice broke. In little more than a whisper he continued, "It is for our safety and our peace. There must be forty lashes; the pain this crime has caused is too great." With his nod, the guards led his mother forward. One gently removed her robe to expose a bony and crooked back. The appointed man stepped forward and began to unwind the whip.

At the same moment, the leader stepped forward and removed his robe as well, exposing his broad shoulders, seasoned and solid. Tenderly, he wrapped his arms around his dear mother, shielding her with his own body.

He whispered gently against her cheek as his tears blended with hers. He nodded once more, and the whip came down again and again.

A single moment, yet in it love and justice found an eternal harmony.

Are You God?

Charles Swindoll

Shortly after World War II came to a close, Europe began picking up the pieces. Much of the Old Country had been ravaged by war and was in ruins. Perhaps the saddest sight of all was that of little orphaned children starving in the streets of those war-torn cities.

Early one chilly morning, an American soldier was making his way back to the barracks in London. As he turned the corner in his jeep, he spotted a little lad with his nose pressed to the window of a pastry shop. Inside, the cook was kneading dough for a fresh batch of doughnuts. The hungry boy stared in silence, watching every move. The soldier pulled his jeep to the curb, stopped, got out, and walked quietly over to where the little fellow was standing. Through the steamed-up window he could see the mouth-watering morsels as they were being pulled from the oven, piping hot. The boy salivated and released a slight groan as he watched the cook place them onto the glass enclosed counter ever so carefully.

The soldier's heart went out to the nameless orphan as he stood beside him.

"Son...would you like some of those?"

The boy was startled.

"Oh, yeah...I would!"

The American stepped inside and bought a dozen, put them in a bag, and walked back to where the lad was standing in the foggy cold of the London morning. He smiled, held out the bag, and said simply: "Here you are."

As he turned to walk away, he felt a tug on his coat. He looked back and heard the child ask quietly, *"Mister...are you God?"*

Words Must Wait

Ruth Bell Graham

Don't talk to me yet;
the wound is fresh,
the nauseous pain
I can't forget
fades into numbness
like a wave,
then comes again.
Your tears I understand,
But grief is deaf;
It cannot hear the words
you gently planned
and tried to say.
But...
pray....

Encouragement

THE SECRET

Someday I hope to enjoy enough of what the world calls success so that somebody will ask me, "What's the secret of it?" I shall say simply this: "I get up when I fall down."

Paul Harvey

Mr. Roth

Author Unknown

An old man showed up at the back door of the house we were renting. Opening the door a few cautious inches, we saw his eyes were glassy and his furrowed face glistened with silver stubble. He clutched a wicker basket holding a few unappealing vegetables. He bid us good morning and offered his produce for sale. We were uneasy enough to make a quick purchase to alleviate both our pity and our fear.

To our chagrin, he returned the next week, introducing himself as Mr. Roth, the man who lived in the shack down the road. As our fears subsided, we got close enough to realize that it wasn't alcohol, but cataracts, that marbleized his eyes. On subsequent visits, he would shuffle in, wearing two mismatched right shoes, and pull out a harmonica. With glazed eyes set on a future glory, he'd puff out old gospel tunes between conversations about vegetables and religion.

On one visit, he exclaimed, "The Lord is so good! I came out of my shack this morning and found a bag full of shoes and clothing on my porch."

"That's wonderful, Mr. Roth," we said. "We're happy for you."

"You know what's even more wonderful?" he asked. "Just yesterday I met some people that could use them."

I Don't Believe a Word of It

Howard Hendricks

By the fifth grade, I was bearing all the fruit of a kid who feels insecure, unloved, and pretty angry at life. In other words, I was tearing the place apart. However, my teacher Miss Simon apparently thought that I was blind to this problem, because she regularly reminded me, "Howard, you are the worst behaved child in this school!"

So tell me something I don't already know! I thought to myself, as I proceeded to live up (or down) to her opinion of me....

Needless to say, the fifth grade was probably the worst year of my life. Finally I was graduated—for obvious reasons. But I left with Miss Simon's words ringing in my ears: "Howard, you are the worst behaved child in this school!"

You can imagine what my expectations were upon entering the sixth grade. The first day of class, my teacher, Miss Noe, went down the roll call, and it wasn't long before she came to my name. "Howard Hendricks," she called out, glancing from her list to where I was sitting with my arms folded, just waiting to go into action. She looked me over for a moment, and then said, "I've heard a lot about you." Then she smiled and added, "But I don't believe a word of it!"

I tell you, that moment was a fundamental turning point, not only in my education, but in my life. Suddenly, unexpectedly, someone believed in me. For the first time in my life, someone saw potential in me. Miss Noe put me on special assignments. She gave me little jobs to do. She invited me to come in after school to work on my reading and arithmetic. She challenged me with higher standards.

I had a hard time letting her down. In fact, one time I got

so involved in one of her homework assignments that I stayed up until 1:30 in the morning working on it! Eventually my father came down the hall and said, "What's the matter son? Are you sick?"

"No, I'm doing my homework," I replied.

He kind of blinked and rubbed his eyes, not quite sure whether he was awake. He'd never heard me say anything like that before....

What made the difference between fifth grade and sixth? The fact that someone was willing to give me a chance. Someone was willing to believe in me while challenging me with higher expectations. That was risky, because there was no guarantee that I would honor Miss Noe's trust.

Everyone likes the end product of mentoring, especially when it yields a peak performer—the star athlete, the successful businessperson, the brilliant lawyer, the impressive communicator. But how many of us want to deal with the person at the front end of the process?

A Perfect Pot of Tea

Roberta Messner

An impatient crowd of nearly 200 diehard bargain hunters shoved their way into the huge living room of the old Withers' homestead. The sweltering 90-degree temperature didn't deter a single one, all in pursuit of the estate sale find of the summer.

The lady conducting the sale, a long-time acquaintance, nodded as we watched the early morning scavengers. "How's this for bedlam?" she chuckled.

I smiled in agreement. "I shouldn't even be here. I have to be at the airport in less than an hour," I admitted to her. "But when I was a teenager, I sold cosmetics in this neighborhood. And Hillary Withers was my favorite customer."

"Then run and check out the attic," she suggested. "There are plenty of old cosmetics up there."

Quickly, I squeezed through the ever-growing throng and climbed the stairs to the third floor. The attic was deserted except for a petite elderly woman presiding over several tables loaded with yellowed bags of all sizes.

"What brings you all the way up here?" she asked as she popped the stopper out of a perfume bottle. "There's nothing up here except old Avon, Tupperware, and Fuller Brush products."

I drew in a long, cautious breath. The unmistakable fragrance of "Here's My Heart" perfume transported me back nearly 20 years.

"Why, this is my own handwriting!" I exclaimed as my eyes fell upon an invoice stapled to one of the bags. The untouched sack held more than a hundred dollars' worth of creams and colognes. This had been my very first sale to Mrs. Withers.

On that long-ago June day, I'd canvassed the wide, tree-lined avenue for nearly four hours, but not one lady-of-the-house had invited me inside. As I rang the bell at the last house, I braced myself for the now-familiar rejection.

"Hello, Ma'am, I'm your new Avon representative," I stammered, when the carved-oak door swung open. "I have some great products I'd like to show you." When my eyes finally found the courage to face the lady in the doorway, I realized it was Mrs. Withers, the bubbly, matronly soprano in our church choir. I'd admired her lovely dresses and hats, dreaming that someday I'd wear stylish clothes, too. Just two months before, when I'd traveled to a distant city to have brain surgery, Mrs. Withers had showered me with the most beautiful cards.

"Why, Roberta, dear, come in, come in," Mrs. Withers' voice sang out. "I need a million and one things. I'm so glad you came to see me."

Gingerly, I eased myself onto the spotless white sofa and unzipped my tweed satchel filled with all the cosmetic samples five dollars could buy. When I handed Mrs. Withers a sales brochure, suddenly I felt like the most important girl in the world.

"Mrs. Withers, we have two types of creams, one for ruddy skin tones and another for sallow skin," I explained with new-found confidence. "And they're great for wrinkles, too."

"Oh good, good," she chirped.

"Which one would you like to try?" I asked, adjusting the wig hiding my stubbly surgery-scarred scalp.

"Oh, I'll surely need one of each," she answered. "And what do you have in the way of fragrances?"

"Here, try this one, Mrs. Withers. They recommend that you place it on the pulse point for the best effect," I instructed, pointing to her diamond-and-gold clad wrist.

"Why, Roberta, you're so knowledgeable about all of this.

You must have studied for days. What an intelligent young woman you are!"

"You really think so, Mrs. Withers?"

"Oh, I know so. And just what do you plan to do with your earnings?"

"I'm saving for college to be a registered nurse," I replied, surprised at my own words. "But today, I'm thinking more of buying my mother a cardigan sweater for her birthday. She always goes with me for my medical treatments, and when we travel on the train, a sweater would be nice for her."

"Wonderful, Roberta, and so considerate. Now what do you have in the gift line?" she asked, requesting two of each item I recommended.

Her extravagant order totaled $117.42. Had she meant to order so much? I wondered. But she smiled back and said, "I'll be looking forward to receiving my delivery, Roberta. Did you say next Tuesday?"

I was preparing to leave when Mrs. Withers said, "You look absolutely famished. Would you like some tea before you go? At our house, we think of tea as 'liquid sunshine.'"

I nodded, then followed Mrs. Withers to her pristine kitchen, filled with all manner of curiosities. I watched, spellbound, as she orchestrated a tea party—like I'd seen in the movies—just for me. She carefully filled the tea kettle with cold water, brought it to a "true" boil, then let the tea leaves steep for exactly five long minutes. "So the flavor will blossom," she explained.

Then she arranged a silver tray with a delicate china tea set, a chintz tea cozy, tempting strawberry scones, and other small splendors. At home, we sometimes drank iced tea in jelly glasses, but never had I felt like a princess invited to afternoon tea.

"Excuse me, Mrs. Withers, but isn't there a faster way to fix tea?" I asked. "At home, we use tea bags."

Mrs. Withers wrapped her arm around my shoulder. "There are some things in life that shouldn't be hurried," she confided. "I've learned that brewing a proper pot of tea is a lot like living a proper life. It takes extra effort, but it's always worth it.

"Take you, for instance, with all of your health problems. Why, you're steeped with determination and ambition, just like a perfect pot of tea. Many people in your shoes would give up, but not you. You can accomplish anything you set your mind to, Roberta."

Abruptly, my journey back in time ended when the lady in the hot, sticky attic asked, "You knew Hillary Withers, too?"

I wiped a stream of perspiration from my forehead. "Yes... I once sold her some of these cosmetics. But I can't understand why she never used them or gave them away."

"She did give a lot of them away," the lady replied matter-of-factly. "But somehow, some of them got missed and ended up here."

"But why did she buy them and not use them?" I asked.

"Oh, she purchased a special brand of cosmetics for her own use." The lady spoke in a confidential whisper. "Hillary had a soft spot in her heart for door-to-door salespeople. She never turned any of them away. She used to tell me, 'I could just give them money, but money alone doesn't buy self-respect. So I give them a little of my money, lend a listening ear, and share my love and prayers. You never know how far a little encouragement can take someone.'"

I paused, remembering how my cosmetic sales had soared after I'd first visited Mrs. Withers. I bought my mother the new sweater from my commission on the sale, and I still had enough money for my college fund. I even went on to win several district and national cosmetics-sales awards. Eventually, I put myself through college with my own earnings and realized my dream of becoming a registered nurse. Later, I earned a master's degree and a Ph.D.

"Mrs. Withers really cared for all of these people?" I asked, pointing to the dozens of time-worn delivery bags on the table.

"Oh, yes," she assured me. "She did it without the slightest desire that anyone would ever know."

I paid the cashier for my purchases—the sack of cosmetics I'd sold to Mrs. Withers, and a tiny, heart-shaped gold locket. I threaded the locket onto the gold chain I wore around my neck. Then I headed for the airport; later that afternoon I was addressing a medical convention in New York.

When I arrived in the elegant hotel ballroom, I found my way to the speaker's podium and scanned the sea of faces—health-care specialists from all over the country. Suddenly, I felt as insecure as on that long-ago day, peddling cosmetics in that unfamiliar, affluent neighborhood.

Can I do it? my mind questioned.

My trembling fingers reached upward to the locket. It opened, revealing a picture of Mrs. Withers inside. I again heard her soft but emphatic words: "You can accomplish anything you set your mind to, Roberta."

"Good afternoon," I began slowly. "Thank you for inviting me to speak about putting the care back in health care. It's often said that nursing is love made visible. But this morning I learned an unexpected lesson about the power of quiet love expressed in secret. The kind of love expressed not for show, but for the good it can do in the lives of others. Some of our most important acts of love often go unnoticed. Until they've had some time to steep—for their flavor to blossom."

Then I told my colleagues the story of Hillary Withers. Much to my surprise, there was thunderous applause. And to think, it all began with a perfect pot of tea!

Encouraging Words

Susan Maycinik

Could I speak to the manager?"

My friend's sudden query to our waitress startled me. Our dinner at a popular pizza restaurant had seemed uneventful, and I wondered what Eileen was up to.

The manager appeared at our table a few minutes later. "What can I do for you?" she asked hesitantly, as if she were expecting yet another reprimand from an angry customer.

"I just wanted you to know that our waitress tonight has really been exceptional," Eileen began. Then she described several things our server had done that impressed her.

The manager was obviously relieved—and delighted. So was the waitress, who was standing nearby. The four of us laughed and chatted for a few minutes. Eileen had made the day of two hard-working women...and left an indelible impression on me of the power of positive words.

When we think about our words, it's easy to focus on the ones we'd like to retrieve. Fortunately, however, there are certain phrases that are almost always the right thing to say—words that communicate love and encouragement. Here are a few:

"You do that really well."

"May I pray for you right now?"

"How *are* you, really?"

"What you said helped me."

"I was wrong."

"Thanks for leading/serving."

"Have I offended you?"

"I appreciate the way you _____."

"What can I do to help?"

"Tell me about your day, job, kids...."

"Please forgive me."

"I still love you."

"God is big enough to _____."

"I'm proud of you."

"You're really growing."

"Please come over for dinner."

"I missed you."

"I'm so happy for you."

"I prayed for you today."

"That must be very difficult."

"I'll be glad to!"

In short, if there are words *you'd* like to hear, it's a good bet they would encourage others, too.

GOD'S PLANS

"For I know the plans I have for you," declares the LORD, *"plans to prosper you and not to harm you, plans to give you hope and a future. Then you will call upon me and come and pray to me, and I will listen to you. You will seek me and find me when you seek me with all your heart."*

JEREMIAH 29:11-13

Three Letters From Teddy

Elizabeth Silance Ballard

Teddy's letter came today and now that I've read it, I will place it in my cedar chest with the other things that are important to my life.

"I wanted you to be the first to know."

I smiled as I read the words he had written and my heart swelled with a pride that I had no right to feel.

I have not seen Teddy Stallard since he was a student in my fifth grade class fifteen years ago. It was early in my career, and I had only been teaching for two years.

From the first day he stepped into my classroom, I disliked Teddy. Teachers (although everyone knows differently) are not supposed to have favorites in a class, but most especially are they not to show dislike for a child, any child.

Nevertheless, every year there are one or two children that one cannot help but be attached to, for teachers are human, and it is human nature to like bright, pretty, intelligent people, whether they are ten years old or twenty-five. And sometimes, not too often, fortunately, there will be one or two students to whom the teacher just can't seem to relate.

I had thought myself quite capable of handling my personal feelings along that line until Teddy walked into my life. There wasn't a child I particularly liked that year, but Teddy was most assuredly the one I disliked.

He was dirty. Not just occasionally, but all the time. His hair hung low over his ears, and he actually had to hold it out of his eyes as he wrote papers in class. (And this was before it was fashionable to do so!) Too, he had a peculiar odor about him which I could never identify.

His physical faults were many, and his intellect left a lot to be desired, also. By the end of the first week I knew he was hopelessly behind the others. Not only was he behind; he was just plain slow! I began to withdraw from him immediately.

Any teacher will tell you that it's more of a pleasure to teach a bright child. It is definitely more rewarding for one's ego. But any teacher worth her credentials can channel work to the bright child, keeping him challenged and learning, while she puts her major effort on the slower ones. Any teacher can do this. Most teachers do it, but I didn't, not that year.

In fact, I concentrated on my best students and let the others follow along as best they could. Ashamed as I am to admit it, I took perverse pleasure in using my red pen; and each time I came to Teddy's paper, the cross marks (and there were many) were always a little larger and a little redder than necessary.

"Poor work!" I would write with a flourish.

While I did not actually ridicule the boy, my attitude was obviously quite apparent to the class, for he quickly became the class "goat," the outcast: the unlovable and the unloved.

He knew I didn't like him, but he didn't know why. Nor did I know—then or now—why I felt such an intense dislike for him. All I know is that he was a little boy no one cared about, and I made no effort on his behalf.

The days rolled by. We made it through the Fall Festival and the Thanksgiving holidays, and I continued marking happily with my red pen.

As the Christmas holidays approached, I knew that Teddy would never catch up in time to be promoted to the sixth grade level. He would be a repeater.

To justify myself, I went to his cumulative folder from time to time. He had very low grades for the first four years, but no grade failure. How he had made it, I didn't know. I closed my mind to the personal remarks.

First grade: Teddy shows promise by work and attitude, but

has poor home situation. Second grade: Teddy could do better. Mother terminally ill. He receives little help at home. Third grade: Teddy is a pleasant boy. Helpful, but too serious. Slow learner. Mother passed away end of the year. Fourth grade: Very slow, but well behaved. Father shows no interest.

Well, they had passed him four times, but he will certainly repeat fifth grade! *Do him good!* I said to myself.

And then the last day before the holiday arrived. Our little tree on the reading table sported paper and popcorn chains. Many gifts were heaped underneath, waiting for the big moment.

Teachers always get several gifts at Christmas, but mine that year seemed bigger and more elaborate than ever. There was not a student who had not brought me one. Each unwrapping brought squeals of delight, and the proud giver would receive effusive thank-yous.

His gift wasn't the last one I picked up; in fact it was in the middle of the pile. Its wrapping was a brown paper bag, and he had colored Christmas trees and red bells all over it. It was stuck together with masking tape.

"For Miss Thompson, from Teddy" it read.

The group was completely silent and for the first time I felt conspicuous, embarrassed because they all stood watching me unwrap the gift.

As I removed the last bit of masking tape, two items fell to my desk: a gaudy rhinestone bracelet with several stones missing and a small bottle of dime-store cologne—half empty.

I could hear the snickers and whispers, and I wasn't sure I could look at Teddy.

"Isn't this lovely?" I asked, placing the bracelet on my wrist. "Teddy, would you help me fasten it?"

He smiled shyly as he fixed the clasp, and I held up my wrist for all of them to admire.

There were a few hesitant ooh's and ahh's, but as I dabbed the cologne behind my ears, all the little girls lined up for a dab behind their ears.

I continued to open gifts until I reached the bottom of the pile. We ate our refreshments, and the bell rang.

The children filed out with shouts of "See you next year!" and "Merry Christmas!" but Teddy waited at his desk.

When they had all left, he walked up to me, clutching his gift and books to his chest.

"You smell just like my mom," he said softly. "Her bracelet looks real pretty on you too. I'm glad you liked it."

He left quickly. I locked the door, sat down at my desk, and wept, resolving to make up to Teddy what I had deliberately deprived him of—a teacher who cared.

I stayed every afternoon with Teddy from the end of Christmas holidays until the last day of school. Sometimes we worked together. Sometimes he worked alone while I drew up lesson plans or graded papers.

Slowly but surely he caught up with the rest of the class. In fact, his final averages were among the highest in the class, and although I knew he would be moving out of the state when school was out, I was not worried for him. Teddy had reached a level that would stand him in good stead the following year, no matter where he went. He had enjoyed a measure of success, and as we were taught in our teacher training courses, "Success builds success."

I did not hear from Teddy until seven years later, when his first letter appeared in my mailbox.

Dear Miss Thompson,
    I just wanted you to be the first to know, I will be graduating second in my class next month.

Very Truly Yours,
Teddy Stallard

I sent him a card of congratulations and a small package, a pen and pencil gift set. I wondered what he would do after graduation.

Four years later, Teddy's second letter came.

Dear Miss Thompson,
I wanted you to be the first to know. I was just informed that I'll be graduating first in my class. The university has not been easy, but I liked it.

Very Truly Yours,
Teddy Stallard

I sent him a good pair of sterling silver monogrammed cuff links and a card, so proud of him I could burst!

And now today—Teddy's third letter.

Dear Miss Thompson,
I wanted you to be the first to know. As of today I am Theodore Stallard, MD. How about that!!??

I'm going to be married in July, the 27th, to be exact. I wanted to ask if you could come and sit where Mom would sit if she were here. I'll have no family there as Dad died last year.

Very Truly Yours,
Teddy Stallard

I'm not sure what kind of gift one sends to a doctor on completion of medical school and state boards. Maybe I'll just wait and take a wedding gift, but a note can't wait.

Dear Ted,
Congratulations! You made it, and you did it yourself!! In spite of those like me and not because of us, this day has come for you.

God bless you. I'll be at the wedding with bells on!

The Comfort of a Cold, Wet Nose

Barbara Baumgardner

I hadn't even wanted the dog in the first place! My husband insisted I get him to replace the dog that had died recently. Soon, he was "my dog," a friend and faithful companion; not asking for any more than I was willing to give—a daily meal, a kind word, a warm bed.

But not my bed! No dogs allowed on my bed.

The night after my husband died, I lay there, staring into the darkness, my pillow soppy wet with the unending flow of tears. The bed seemed so big all by myself and I was wondering how long it takes for a good case of "loneliness" to heal when I first felt it move. It was cold and clammy and creeping at a very slow pace into my open hand outside the covers. The solidified jelly-like mass was followed by prickly hairs and just before I screamed, a muffled but familiar whine came from the creature that was forcing its cold, wet nose into my trembling hand.

"Oh, Shawn! What are you doing on my bed?" I threw my arms around his thick hairy neck and hugged and hugged.

In the days and months to follow, I came to realize that this dog I hadn't wanted was a gift of love from God. He was a warm fuzzy on my bed every night; a companion always willing, wagging, and available to go for a walk when I needed to get out of the house. Twice, he snapped at me as I wailed loudly and out of control, as if to reprimand me to be strong and of good courage.

Shawn taught me all about love and acceptance and forgiveness. That crazy dog loves me just as I am. And so I've learned to be a warm fuzzy to those around me who are hurting and to approach them gently, loving them just as they are. Like my dog curled up by the warm fire, I just want to be there in case I'm needed. I thank God for providing a friend when I felt alone, and for the comfort of a cold, wet nose.

AND THIS, TOO...

It is said an Eastern monarch once charged his wise men to invent him a sentence, to be ever in view,
and which should be true and appropriate in all times and situations.
They presented him the words: "And this, too, shall pass away."
How much it expresses! How chastening in the hour of pride—
how consoling in the depth of affliction!

Abraham Lincoln

Giving and Receiving

Billie Davis

A public school teacher made clear to me the complex ideas of giving and receiving.

Evidently she noticed something about the way I held the book in reading class and arranged for an eye examination. She did not send me to a clinic; she took me to her own oculist, not as a charity case but as a friend. Indeed, I was so intrigued with the activity that I did not realize exactly what had happened until one day at school she gave me the glasses.

"I can't take them. I can't pay for them," I said, embarrassed by my family's poverty.

She told me a story: "When I was a child, a neighbor bought glasses for me. She said I should pay for them someday by getting glasses for some other little girl. So, you see, the glasses were paid for before you were born."

Then the teacher said the most welcome words that anyone had ever said to me: "Someday you will buy glasses for some other little girl."

She saw me as a giver. She made me responsible. She believed I might have something to offer to someone else. She accepted me as a member of the same world she lived in. I walked out of that room, clutching the glasses, not as a recipient of charity, but as a trusted courier.

Teacher Dan

Marilyn McAuley

Hi, teacher Dan!" chorus a roomful of preschoolers.

Dan is a grandfatherly figure with his silver hair, a round smiling face, and blue eyes that reveal a gentle nature. He smiles and greets the children. Twice a week he visits their school briefly on his way to another classroom.

He walks through the garage-turned-preschool into the house and down the hall. He stops at an open door. It's a classroom without blackboards or brightly trimmed bulletin boards. There are no rows of desks and no school bell. Instead, it's a spare bedroom with a large computer desk, a new computer, two chairs, and a sofa.

His student, Jason, is seated at his computer. The dark wavy hair bounces as Jason's whole body impersonates the gyrations of a favorite rock star. Long fingers pound an imaginary piano as he listens to his music.

Dan waits.

Jason is a neat kid. Many would say life hasn't been fair to him. For most of his eighteen years, Jason has been afflicted with seizures. As puberty set in, they increased so in frequency and intensity that he must be tutored at home. His speech is slow and measured. He walks unsteadily. His ability to move his thoughts into words is slowed by the ailment gripping his brain.

A retired special education teacher, Dan still spends two days a week tutoring Jason, who is now a junior in high school and taller than his six-foot teacher. Jason's strong angular jaw line frames a handsome face. He's a tease and enjoys telling jokes. He also has a clear understanding of right and wrong, and his faith in God is strong.

Jason's movements are a bit jerky as he turns to see Dan. They both have an unspoken hope that Jason will get through the ninety-minute class without a seizure.

In his deep, quiet voice he greets his teacher. "Hi, D-an."

"How are you doing today?" Dan asks.

"Gr-eat. I mi-ss-ed you la-st ti-me. I'm g-lad you are w-ell now."

"I would rather have been here than home nursing a cold."

"C-olds are a-ppall-ing."

"Great, Jason. I'm glad to see you are using your vocabulary words. I think 'appalling' is one of your favorites, isn't it?"

Jason grinned. "I like a-ppall-ing."

"Well, shall we get started?"

As any teenager would do, Jason stalls for time. "Did you kn-ow they are-n't ma-k-ing ba-na-nas any long-er?"

"Aw Jason, what do you mean they aren't making bananas any longer—why not?"

Jason laughs and slaps the table. "Be-cau-se, they are l-ong e-nough." He grabs his small towel and wipes a drool from his mouth. His eyes are bright as he watches Dan enjoy the joke.

"You did it again, Jason. I really fell for that one." Dan is so proud of Jason being able to tell the joke and get the punch line right.

After reviewing current events, Jason must write three statements about their discussion. Time passes...five minutes...ten. Nothing happens.

Dan waits.

Looking at Jason's bowed head he says, "Jason, are you thinking about what you want to write?" He doesn't answer but raises his head and looks at the keyboard. Slowly he begins a word. After twenty-five minutes, he has typed his three sentences. Not compound sentences—just simple ones of five to ten words.

Dan listens as Jason reads them back to him. They talk about the changes that could be made. Jason doesn't like to make errors. He tries so hard to be perfect. His mind is alert, it just takes him time to pull his thoughts and words together. Only one word is corrected. They give a high-five. It's a good day.

"Let's look at your homework."

"Ho-me-wor-k is a-ppall-ing!"

"I think you've got that word down perfect."

After lessons, Jason gets to pick an educational computer game to challenge Dan. Again, Jason wins.

"D-an, you h-ave bee-n tea-ching me for al-mo-st two yea-rs."

This is significant for Jason. Dan has brought solidarity into Jason's life—something he needed after having four teachers come and go in one year.

The ninety minutes are up. Dan asks, "What is your homework assignment for Thursday?"

"A-ppall-ing math." They laugh.

Dan picks up his briefcase and Jason follows him to the door.

"I'll see you Thursday."

"B-ye D-an."

Jason stands at the door and waves. He enjoys his time with Dan because he's treated with dignity and respect.

Dan puts the briefcase in the back seat. As he turns around, Jason is coming toward him. The cold misty rain dampens his T-shirt.

"Jason, be careful," Dan cautions with deliberate calm. "Take it slow—don't fall." Jason has just healed from surgery for a broken jaw—the result of a fall.

Jason keeps coming so Dan walks toward him.

He throws his arms around Dan and gives him a big hug.

Jason has never shown such deep feelings. Dan returns the hug and gently guides him back to the house. Heading back to the car Dan hears, "I l-ove you, D-an!"

Teacher Dan drives away. Tears moisten the corners of his eyes. If Jason had been his only student, it was well worth becoming a teacher.

Faith is...
Remembering
I am God's
priceless treasure
when I feel
utterly worthless.

Pamela Reeve

The Mender

Ruth Bell Graham

He had built for himself a great house on one of the Caribbean islands. It is a thing to behold. Tall rusty iron columns, collected and resurrected with an ingenious homemade device. This Great House is a masterpiece of salvaged materials.

A collector and seller of scrap metal as well as antiques, he was also fascinated with broken bits and pieces of china dug from his front yard. His friends, John and June Cash, laughingly remarked it was the first time they had heard of a yard sale where the man had sold the yard itself. Carefully he fitted and glued the pieces together. Few ever came out whole. They remained simply a collection of one who cared.

When I expressed interest, he gave me a blue-and-white plate, carefully glued together—pieces missing.

"You remind me of God," I said. By the look on his face, I knew I shocked him, and I hurriedly explained.

"God pieces back broken lives lovingly. Sometimes a piece is irretrievably lost. But still He gathers what He can and restores us."

Long Range Vision

Howard Hendricks

As a boy I loved to wander over to a nearby park and watch the older men play checkers. One day one of them invited me to play. At first it looked easy. I captured one, then another of his checkers. But then, suddenly, he took one checker and hopped and skipped right across the board to the border and yelled, "King me!" With that king, he proceeded to wipe me off the board.

That day I learned about long-range vision. No one minds losing a few checkers if he's headed for king territory.

There are no hopeless situations in life...
only men who have grown hopeless about them.

A Barclay Comment

The Red Coat

Melody Carlson

The colors of the quilt squares and triangles are poured across her lap like jewels. Patches of golds, greens, and reds. She runs her hand over a block of garnet-red wool, and smiles. That's exactly the color of faith.

* * *

It was a cold windy day, with winter nipping at the heels of fall. She picked up Abby from grade school and they rode the city bus downtown. Abby was bundled in a hand-me-down coat from her cousin, Linda Sue. It was in perfect shape with a rabbit fur collar, and hardly worn. They hopped off the bus and she held Abby's hand as they dashed across the street. The wind whipped up a piece of newspaper and cut right through her thin brown coat—the same coat she'd gotten just before the war. Styles had changed a lot since then, with hemlines going up and down like an elevator. Now there wasn't enough of the coat left to alter one more time and her full skirt peeked out from beneath it like a dust ruffle.

John had been home since September and the only job he'd been able to secure was as a janitor at the hospital. He hoped to start night school in January, education seemed to be the ticket to a better job. Lately he'd scrimped and saved, and just that morning handed over twelve dollars saying, "Now, you go over to Harricks and find yourself a good winter coat." She'd agreed, thinking it would be a challenge to find much of a coat for twelve dollars. She knew he meant well, but it might've been better to put the money under the mattress for a rainy day. Lord knew they'd had plenty of those.

She and Abby entered Harricks and suddenly she remembered how she used to shop there with her mother, back when money flowed freely, before she'd married John against the wishes of her family. Now the shop seemed like a foreign land, and she felt like an intruder.

"May I help you?" asked a plump woman straightening gloves upon the counter.

"No thank you, I just want to look around a bit." No use telling her she was looking for a coat, with only twelve dollars in her purse. The woman might laugh.

She walked through the store, pretending to observe the many pretty things. Abby pointed out a bright peacock blue evening dress. "That would look nice on you, Mommy." She stroked her daughter's sleek brown hair, the same color as her own, and smiled. Finally they reached the back of the store and she turned around, ready to give up. Relief mixed with disappointment. But there nestled in the corner was a rack with various items and a sign that proclaimed, "sale." She glanced at the rack and something red caught her eye. It turned out to be a wool coat in a lovely shade of red, just the color of garnets. She carefully removed the hanger from the rack and searched the coat for a price tag. But surely, even on sale, it would cost too much.

"Mommy, the tag says twelve dollars!" Abby triumphantly held up the sleeve with the bright yellow tag. "You can get it, Mommy, that's just the right price."

"Oh, that can't possibly be right. It's much too nice. There must be some mistake."

"Try it on, Mommy. See if it fits." Abby tugged at the sleeve of her old coat.

"It's probably not even my size." But in the same moment, she laid down her old coat and slipped into the red coat. She couldn't explain why, but it felt like honey. It was delicious.

"It's perfect, Mommy. And it's beautiful! You look like a princess." Abby pushed her toward the mirror. It looked fine, probably too fine. And perhaps the red, though lovely, was too bright for a woman almost thirty. She hung the coat back on the hanger, then held it at arm's length to study it again. It was a nice design with bound button holes and large abalone buttons. Even the lining was smooth heavy satin—that's why it felt like honey.

"Are you going to buy it, Mommy?"

"Oh, I don't know, Abby. I think there's a mistake. This is a very well-made coat. The price tag can't be right. Coats like this don't end up on the clearance rack, especially in November."

"It says twelve dollars, it must be right." Abby folded her arms and tapped her size two shoe with impatience. "Daddy said you're supposed to get a coat. Now you better get it."

She smiled down at Abby, then laid the coat over her arm and headed for the counter. An elderly woman was being waited on. The sales clerk carefully placed a brown felt hat with a long black feather into a hat box and rang up the price. The cash register jingled as the tray popped open.

"That'll be thirty-two dollars," announced the clerk, and the woman wrote out a check without even blinking. She picked up her pretty box and bid the clerk good day.

"Can I help you?" asked the clerk sweetly. Her hand was extended as she reached expectantly for the coat.

"No, I uh, I think I'd like to look around just a little more." She stepped back and studied the coat again. The price tag was a mistake. If a silly hat sold for thirty-two dollars, how could this beautiful coat be twelve?

"What are you doing, Mommy?" complained Abby as she followed her back to the sales rack.

"Honey, I just know it's a mistake. You can't buy a coat like this for twelve dollars. There's no point in even asking. We'll just look silly."

"But the tag says—"

"Shhh, honey, don't make a scene." She looked around. Several other shoppers were close by now. She recognized Lily Andrews from church. She was new in town and her husband was a doctor. Mrs. Andrews smiled their way, and moved toward the sales rack. It seemed strange that someone so well off would be interested in clearance items. Her hand paused on the red coat and she pulled it from the rack.

"May I help you?" asked the clerk.

"What a lovely coat. And only twelve dollars?"

"That's right. It was from last year; someone returned it in July if you can believe that. A woman kept it all winter and never wore it. She never even took the tags off. The store owner just wanted to get rid of this coat since it doesn't fit with the new line up in front. It's quite a bargain—"

She couldn't hear any more. She took Abby's hand and quickly led her out.

"But Mommy, that's your coa—"

"Shh, honey...."

Tears stung her eyes as the wind blew even colder outside. It was still too early for the return bus, but they settled down on the bus stop bench to wait anyway. They huddled together for warmth.

"Why didn't you get your coat, Mommy?" Abby's voice was sad.

"I don't know, honey...."

How could she tell her it was because she was foolish? And not only was she foolish, she was too proud to ask. How could she explain to John that their eight-year-old daughter had more sense than she did. She shivered. She deserved another winter in her old worn out coat. That would teach her a lesson!

"Excuse me," called a voice. She looked up to see Lily Andrews.

"Yes?"

"I know this is going to sound very strange. And believe me I don't usually do things like this, but I just got the strongest impression to give you this. I have no idea why—" She thrust the package toward them.

"I don't understand—"

"Neither do I. But it's as if God told me to do this. I know it's very strange, you probably think I'm crazy—"

"It is strange." She peeked in the bag. "I almost bought this coat just a few minutes ago. Please let me pay you for it." She grabbed eagerly for her purse.

"No, that's just it. I got the impression I was to give it to you. You cannot pay me for it. I'm sorry. I must sound like a mad woman…." Her face was red, and tears were in her eyes.

"But I can't take this, it's like charity."

"No, it's not charity. Go ahead and give your money to someone who needs it if you like. But I know I'm supposed to give this to you. I'm sorry if I sound nutty, maybe I'm just lonely, but it's the first time I ever thought I heard God tell me to do something. You have to let me do it. Think of it as a gift from God. Like faith."

* * *

That was over four decades ago. She'd worn the coat for many winters. Finally it was so out of style that even Abby pleaded with her to give it up, but she could never bring herself to part with it. It had been packed in a trunk for ages, and she'd only thought of it last week when Dr. Andrews passed away and she wanted to do something special for her friend Lily. Now she was carefully cutting the pieces into a lap quilt for her good friend. She hoped it might be a comfort and a reminder that faith can be found in small things like red wool coats, and friendships that endure throughout time.

The Young Widow

Alice Gray

Her husband died suddenly in an accident and she was left to raise her two sons alone. At first she was surrounded by compassionate and caring friends. They brought meals, sent cards, made phone calls, prayed. And then the weeks turned into months, and it seemed like all the world had forgotten. She longed to hear her husband's name mentioned in conversation, she longed to talk about the wide stride of his walk, the warmth of his easy laugh, and how his hand had felt so strong in hers. She wanted the neighbors to come and borrow his tools or have a grown man shoot basketballs with her sons.

It was early on the morning of the first anniversary of his death. The dew was still wet on the grass as she walked across the cemetery lawn. And then she saw it, laying next to his gravestone. Someone had been there even before her and left a small bouquet of fresh cut flowers, tied with a ribbon. A gentle caring act that reached out to her lonely heart like a tender hug. With tears streaming down her cheeks, she read the unsigned note. The three words said simply, "I remember, too."

Michael's Story Begins at Age Six

Charlotte Elmore

In desperation, I asked if he could be retested. She shook her head and said no. In an attempt to show her just how "normal" Michael really was, I began telling her about all the things that Michael did well. But she brushed my comments aside and stood up, dismissing me. "Michael will be all right," she said.

Later that evening, after Michael and his three-year-old sister, Linda, were in bed, I tearfully told Frank what I had learned that day. After talking it over, we agreed that we knew our son much better than an IQ test. We decided that Michael's low score must have been a mistake.

Like me, Frank could not believe that our son was "nearly retarded." Instead, he told me about some of the things Michael recently had done that he felt proved Michael was intelligent.... He said that one night Michael showed an interest in the blueprint sketches he was working on, so he found Michael's set of odd-shaped blocks and quickly sketched two-dimensional drawings of each of them. Frank then asked Michael to match each block with its corresponding drawing. Frank said he was pleased with how easily Michael made things with his toy construction sets from the diagrams that came with the toys.

We moved to Fort Wayne, Indiana, in 1962, and Michael entered Concordia Lutheran High School. His grades warranted his selecting college preparatory courses, including biology, Latin, and algebra—the subject we had been told, when he was back in first grade, he would never be able to handle. Biology soon became his favorite subject. He started telling everyone he was going to be a doctor.

Michael entered Indiana University at Bloomington in 1965 as a premedical student. By midyear, with a 3.47 grade point average, he had made the dean's list, and his faculty counselor gave him special permission to take more than the recommended number of course hours. He earned enough credits to be accepted into the Indiana University School of Medicine in Indianapolis at the end of his junior year in college.

During his first year at medical school, Michael took another IQ test and scored 126, an increase of 36 points. An increase like that was supposed to be impossible.

On graduation day, May 21, 1972, Frank, Linda, and I attended the ceremony and hugged our Dr. Mike! After the ceremony, we told Michael and Linda about the low IQ score Michael had received when he was six—as we had planned to do all along. At first, both of them thought we were joking. Since that day, Michael sometimes will look at us and say with a big grin, "My parents never told me that I couldn't be a doctor—that is, not until after I graduated from medical school!" It's his way of thanking us for the faith we had in him.

It has been said that children often live up to what adults expect of them—tell a child he is "dumb" and he may play the part. We often wonder what would have happened if we had treated Michael as "nearly retarded" and imposed a limit on his dreams.

Come in Together

Stu Weber

We'd been running every day, but this was something else. We'd been sweating from the time we rolled out of the rack before daybreak, but now moisture drained from every pore in our bodies. Sure, this was the physical training stage of U.S. Army Ranger school, and we expected exertion. Even exhaustion. But this was no morning PT rah-rah run in T-shirts.

We ran in full field uniform. As usual, the word was "You go out together, you stick together, you work as a unit, and you come in together. If you don't come in together, don't bother to come in!"

Somewhere along the way, through a fog of pain, thirst, and fatigue, my brain registered something strange about our formation. Two rows ahead of me, I noticed one of the guys out of sync.

A big, rawboned redhead named Sanderson. His legs were pumping, but he was out of step with the rest of us. Then his head began to loll from side to side. This guy was struggling. Close to losing it.

Without missing a step, the Ranger on Sanderson's right reached over and took the distressed man's rifle. Now one of the Rangers was packing two weapons. His own and Sanderson's. The big redhead did better for a time. But then, while the platoon kept moving. His jaw became slack, his eyes glazed and his legs pushed like pistons. Soon his head began to sway again.

This time, the Ranger on the left reached over, removed Sanderson's helmet, tucked it under his own arm, and continued to run. All systems go. Our boots thudded along the dirt trail in heavy unison. Tromp-tromp-tromp-tromp-tromp-tromp.

Sanderson was hurting. Really hurting. He was buckling, going down. But no. Two soldiers behind him lifted the pack off his back, each taking a shoulder strap in his free hand. Sanderson gathered his remaining strength. Squared his shoulders. And the platoon continued to run. All the way to the finish line.

We left together. We returned together. And all of us were the stronger for it.

Together is better.

Life is teaching you some painful lessons.
But it is from adversity that strength is born.
You may have lost the inning, but I know you'll win the game.

from P.S. I Love You

First Things

Tony Campolo

When I was a kid growing up, I knew a man who loomed bigger than life to me. His name was Edwin E. Bailey, and he ran the astronomical observatory at the Franklin Institute in Philadelphia. I would go to the Franklin Institute most Saturdays just to spend time with him. His encyclopedic mind fascinated me. He seemed to know something about everything.

I was friends with Ed Bailey right up until he died several years ago. When he was in the hospital, after a serious stroke, I went to visit him. In an effort to make small talk, I told about all the places I had been to speak and how I had come to his bedside right from the airport.

He heard me out and then said with a slightly sarcastic manner, "You go all over the world to people who, ten years from now, won't remember your name. But you haven't left time for the people who really care about you."

That simple sentence hit me hard and changed my life. I have decided not to let my time be used up by people to whom I make no difference, while I neglect those for whom I am irreplaceable.

A friend of mine recently got a call from the White House asking him to consult with the President of the United States. He said no because it was to be on a day he had promised to spend with his granddaughter at the seashore. The nation survived without him, the President didn't miss him, and his granddaughter had some precious time with her "Pop-Pop." First things ought to be put first.

Virtue

FORGIVENESS

Forgiveness is like the violet
Sending forth its pure fragrance
On the heel of the boot
Of the one who crushed it.

Author Unknown

These Things I Wish for You

Paul Harvey

We tried so hard to make things better for our kids that we made them worse.

For my grandchildren, I'd know better.

I'd really like for them to know about hand-me-down clothes and homemade ice cream and leftover meat loaf. I really would.

My cherished grandson, I hope you learn humility by being humiliated and that you learn honesty by being cheated.

I hope you learn to make your bed and mow the lawn and wash the car—and I hope nobody gives you a brand-new car when you are 16.

And I hope you have a job by then.

It will be good if at least one time you can see a baby calf born and see your old dog put to sleep.

I hope you get a black eye fighting for something you believe in.

I hope you have to share a bedroom with your younger brother. And it is all right to draw a line down the middle of the room, but—when he wants to crawl under the covers with you because he's scared—I hope you'll let him.

And when you want to see a Disney movie and your kid brother wants to tag along I hope you take him.

I hope you have to walk uphill with your friends and that you live in a town where you can do it safely.

And rainy days when you have to hitch a ride I hope your driver doesn't have to drop you two blocks away so you won't be seen riding with somebody as uncool as your mom.

If you want a slingshot I hope your father teaches you how to make one instead of buy one. I hope you learn to dig in the dirt and read books, and when you learn to use those new-fangled computers, you also learn how to add and subtract in your head.

I hope you get razzed by friends when you have your first crush on a girl, and that when you talk back to your mother I hope you learn what Ivory soap tastes like.

May you skin your knee climbing a mountain, burn your hand on the stove and stick your tongue on a frozen flagpole.

I hope you get sick when some stupid old person blows cigar smoke in your face. I don't care if you try beer once, but I hope you won't like it. And if a friend offers you a joint or any dope I hope you are smart enough to realize he is not your friend.

I sure hope you make time to sit on a porch with your grandpa or go fishing with your uncle. May you feel sorrow at a funeral and the joy of holidays.

I hope your mother punishes you when you throw a baseball through a neighbor's window and that she hugs you and kisses you at Christmas time, when you give her a plaster of Paris mold of your hand.

These things I wish for you—tough times and disappointment, hard work and happiness.

Why I'm a Sports Mom

Judy Bodmer

I t's a Saturday in May. I could be home, curled up on the couch with a good mystery. Instead I'm sitting on a cold metal bench in the stands of a baseball park. An icy wind creeps through my winter jacket. I blow on my hands wishing I'd brought my woolen mittens.

"Mrs. Bodmer?" It's my son's coach. "I thought you'd like to know. We're going to start your son today in right field. He's worked hard this year. We think he deserves the opportunity."

"Thanks," I say feeling proud of my son who has given this man and this team everything he has. I know how bad he wants to start. I'm glad his hard work is being rewarded.

Suddenly I'm nervous for him. I go to the concession stand and buy hot chocolate. Back in my seat I hold it between my hands blowing the steam into my face for warmth.

The team, in their white and blue pinstripe uniforms, struts onto the field. They all look so much alike. I search for my son's number. It isn't there. Instead, Eddie takes right field. I look again, unbelieving. Yes, it's Eddie, the most inexperienced player on the team. How can that be? I glance at the coach, but he's absorbed in the game. I want to run over and ask what's going on, but I know my son wouldn't like that. Over the last eight years I've learned the proper etiquette for moms, and talking to the coach during the game is definitely not acceptable.

My son grips the chain link fence, which protects the bench from stray balls, and yells encouragement to his teammates. I try to read his nonverbals, but I know he has learned, like most men, to hide his feelings from the world.

My heart breaks. So much hard work, so much disappointment. I don't understand what drives young boys to put themselves through this.

"Atta boy, Eddie," yells someone nearby. It's Eddie's father. I can see him smiling, proud his son is starting. I shake my head because I've seen this same man walk out of games when his son dropped a ball or made a bad throw. But for now, he's proud. His son is starting. My son is on the bench.

By the fourth inning my fingers are stiff from the cold, and my feet are numb, but I don't care. My son has been called into the game and he's about to come up to bat. I glance at the dugout. He stands, sorts through the batting helmets and chooses one. Please, I pray, let him get a hit. He picks a bat and struts to the batter's box. I grip the metal seat as he takes a couple of practice swings, adjusts his batting glove and steps up to the plate. The pitcher looks like an adult. I wonder if anyone has checked his birth certificate.

Strike one. "Nice swing!" I yell.

The next pitch is a ball. "Good eye! Good eye!"

Strike two.

The pitcher winds up for the throw. I hold my breath.

Strike three. My son's head hangs and he slowly walks back to the dugout. I look away knowing there's nothing I can do.

For eight years I've been sitting here. I've drunk gallons of terrible coffee, eaten my share of green hot-dogs and salty popcorn. I've suffered from the cold and the heat, eaten dust, and sat in the rain.

Some people wonder why a sane person would go through this. It's not because I want to fulfill my dreams of excelling at sports through my children. And I also don't do this because of the emotional highs. Oh yes, there have been a few. I've seen one or the other of my sons score the winning goal in soccer and hit home runs in baseball and spark a come-from-behind in basketball. But mostly I've seen heartache.

I've waited at home with them for a phone call telling them

they'd made the team. Phone calls that never came. I've seen them sit on the bench game after game and get up to bat only to strike out. I've sat in emergency rooms as their broken bones were set and swollen ankles x-rayed. I've watched coaches yell at them. I've sat here year after year observing it all and wondering why.

The game is over. I stretch my legs and try to stomp life back into my frozen feet. The coach meets with the team. They yell some rallying cry and then descend on their parents. I notice Eddie's dad is slapping him on the back with a big grin on his face. My son wants money for a hamburger. While I wait, the coach approaches me. I can't bring myself to look at him.

"Mrs. Bodmer, I wanted you to know that's a fine young man you have there."

"Why?" I ask, waiting for him to explain why he broke my son's heart.

"When I told your son he could start, he thanked me and then turned me down. He told me to let Eddie start, that it meant more to him."

I turn to watch my son stuffing a burger into his mouth. I realize then why I sit in the stands. Where else can I watch my son grow into a man?

To Whom Shall I Leave My Kingdom?

Donald E. Wildmon

Once the King of a large kingdom was growing old. He decided that it was time to select an heir from among his four sons, so he called them in one at a time to discuss the inheritance of his kingdom.

When the first son entered the chamber of the King and sat down, the King spoke to him. "My son, I am very old and will not live much longer. I wish to entrust my kingdom to the son best suited to receive it. Tell me, if I leave my kingdom to you what will you give to the kingdom?"

Now this son was very rich. So when asked the question, he replied: "I am a man of vast wealth. If you leave me your kingdom I will give it all of my wealth and it will be the richest kingdom in all the world."

"Thank you, son," the King said as he dismissed the son.

When the second son entered, the King spoke to him. "My son, I am very old and will not live much longer. I wish to entrust my kingdom to the son best suited to receive it. Tell me, if I leave my kingdom to you what will you give to the kingdom?"

Now this son was very intelligent. So when asked the question, he replied: "I am a man of vast intelligence. If you leave me your kingdom I will give it all of my intelligence and it will be the most intelligent kingdom in all the world."

"Thank you, son," the King said as he dismissed the son.

When the third son entered, the King spoke to him. "My son, I am very old and will not live much longer. I wish to entrust my kingdom to the son best suited to receive it. Tell me, if I leave my kingdom to you what will you give to the kingdom?"

Now this son was very strong. So when asked the question, he replied: "I am a man of great strength. If you leave me your kingdom I will give it all of my strength and it will be the strongest kingdom in all the world."

"Thank you, son," the King said as he dismissed the son.

The fourth son entered and was greeted by the King in the same fashion as the other three. "My son, I am very old and will not live much longer. I wish to entrust my kingdom to the son best suited to receive it. Tell me, if I leave my kingdom to you what will you give to the kingdom?"

Now this son wasn't especially rich, or smart, or strong. So he replied, "My father, you know that my brothers are much richer, smarter and stronger than I. While they have spent years gaining these attributes, I have spent my time among the people in your kingdom. I have shared with them in their sickness and sorrow. And I have learned to love them. I'm afraid that the only thing I have to give to your kingdom is my love of the people. I know that my brothers have more to offer than I do, therefore I will not be disappointed in not being named your heir. I will simply go on doing what I have always done."

When the king died the people anxiously awaited the news as to their new ruler. And the greatest rejoicing the kingdom ever knew took place when the fourth son was named by the King as his successor.

The MagnaDoodle Message

Liz Curtis Higgs

Every seat was filled as we waited in the county clerk's office to get my driver's license renewed. Children of all ages wandered about exploring their temporary environment, as did my own wee ones.

Lillian was a lap baby at the time (although she never stayed there), and Matthew was four and already beginning to write recognizable words. He never went anywhere without his MagnaDoodle drawing toy, and that morning was no exception.

I encouraged my sometimes-shy son to venture out to the center of the room where several kids were playing with a stack of books and games. Matthew went, dragging his MagnaDoodle behind him. A younger child was turning the pages of a colorful book, which Matthew soon became interested in too. A minute later, my son wrestled the book out of the other child's fingers and was enjoying the brightly colored pages all by himself, leaving the little boy out of the fun.

Until that moment, I had merely watched this little drama unfold; now it was time to enter the scene. "Matthew!" I whispered sharply. "That was not nice. Please apologize and give him back his book right away."

Looking miserable, Matthew extended the much-prized book in the tot's direction, to which the little boy responded with the toddler version of "Harrumph!" and tottered away.

Now Matthew was *really* miserable; he'd upset his mother, and now some kid was unhappy with him too. Matthew sat for a moment, staring into space while the wheels turned inside. Then slowly picking up his MagnaDoodle, he wrote something down and without a word, held it up for the other child to see.

The toddler ignored him, of course, because he couldn't read the words.

But I could. "I'm sorry," it said. So simple, so profound. Matthew couldn't bring himself to speak the words, but he could put it in writing. When the boy didn't respond as Matthew hoped, he held up the sign again, holding it out farther, with a pleading expression on his face, but to no avail.

Around the room, other mothers were beginning to notice the quiet four-year-old with wheat-colored hair and a little sign that read, "I'm sorry." I wasn't the only one who had to blink back tears.

A man never discloses his own character so clearly as when he describes another's.

Jean Paul Richter
1763-1825

Beauty Contest

Carla Muir

A successful beauty product company asked the people in a large city to send pictures along with brief letters about the most beautiful women they knew. Within a few weeks thousands of letters were delivered to the company.

One letter in particular caught the attention of the employees and soon it was handed to the company president. The letter was written by a young boy who was obviously from a broken home, living in a run-down neighborhood. With spelling corrections, an excerpt from his letter read: "A beautiful woman lives down the street from me. I visit her every day. She makes me feel like the most important kid in the world. We play checkers and she listens to my problems. She understands me and when I leave she always yells out the door that she's proud of me."

The boy ended his letter saying, "This picture shows you that she is the most beautiful woman. I hope I have a wife as pretty as her."

Intrigued by the letter, the president asked to see this woman's picture. His secretary handed him a photograph of a smiling, toothless woman, well-advanced in years, sitting in a wheelchair. Sparse gray hair was pulled back in a bun and wrinkles that formed deep furrows on her face were somehow diminished by the twinkle in her eyes.

"We can't use this woman," explained the president, smiling. "She would show the world that our products aren't necessary to be beautiful."

Bouquet

David Seamands

Someone once asked Corrie ten Boom how she could possibly handle all the compliments and praise that were constantly heaped upon her, without becoming proud. She said she looked at each compliment as a beautiful long-stemmed flower given to her. She smelled it for a moment and then put it into a vase with the others. Each night, just before retiring, she took the beautiful bouquet and handed it over to God saying, "Thank you, Lord, for letting me smell the flowers; they all belong to you." She had discovered the secret to genuine humility.

If you're headed in the wrong direction,
God allows U-Turns.

From a bumper sticker

Olympic Gold

Catherine Swift

Saturday, July 5, 1924, was the day for the 8th Olympiad of modern times to begin. After the first modern games were played in Greece in 1896, as a tribute to the French Baron who revived them, the Olympics were staged in Paris. Compared to the first Olympics when thirteen countries took part, this time there were forty-five countries and the stadium was filled with 60,000 spectators.

Amid the waving and cheering there came the skirl of the pipes, and the Queen's Cameron Highlanders emerged from the gateway. They were an impressive sight in their swinging kilts and bearskin headdresses. For a moment the crowd seemed mesmerized at the sight and sound, but when the team from Great Britain came marching in behind the band, the cheers rang out even louder....

The Olympic relay torch wasn't a part of the ceremony in those days, but thousands of pigeons were released to wing their way over the entire country with the good news.

After this the Olympic Oath was recited, and then the four thousand competitors filed out of the arena again to more wild cheering and waving. The 8th Olympiad had begun. All this while Eric Liddell was coming under a lot of pressure to run in the 100 meters. Really it hadn't stopped from that day months earlier when he said he wouldn't run on a Sunday. But once in Paris the criticism began to hurt more.

Eric went to see Harold Abrahams, Britain's remaining hope for a medal in the 100 meters, and he wished him well. As a Jew, Harold's Sabbath was Saturday and Eric respected this. He understood that it was as right for Harold to run on a Sunday as it would have been wrong for himself.

Sunday, July 6, saw the young Cambridge University student Abrahams lined up for the 100-meter preliminary heat. At the same time, Eric Liddell was addressing a congregation in the Scots Kirk (church) on the other side of Paris.

Harold came through both heats. The following day he was all set for the semi-final, and among the spectators was Eric to cheer him on to victory. Then came the final and it was a tremendous victory for Harold. He reached the tape in 10.6 seconds. The stadium erupted in loud applause. No European had ever won a gold medal in that event, and it would be fifty-six years before one won it again.

Deep inside, Eric must have felt a tinge of regret—but there wasn't an element of envy in him. He was elated for Harold's success.

Now he felt free of the criticism too and was able to concentrate on his own two events. The heats for the 200-meter race were held on Tuesday. Both Eric and Harold qualified in each for a place in the final the next day.

Wednesday was another searingly hot day. Eric was lined up with Harold and four Americans. Both British men got off to a good start, but first one and then the other fell behind. Two of the Americans reached the tape first, taking the gold and the silver medals. Eric placed third, and Harold came in sixth and last place.

This may seem disastrous, but it was really a success for Eric. Scotland had never won a bronze for the 200-meter race. And the whole of Britain had never achieved anything better than third place and a bronze medal.

But when Thursday came and the 400-meter heats, Eric didn't do too badly. He didn't shine, either, even though his time improved in each heat. It was better still the next day in the semi-final. Still, he only managed to qualify. On the previous day, in one heat, Imbach of Switzerland actually broke the world record when he ran the distance in 48 seconds.

There were six finalists: two Americans, one Canadian, and the two Britishers, Guy Butler and Eric Liddell....

As usual, Eric went along the line shaking the competitors' hands and giving them his best wishes. This was a ritual the international crown had begun to look for although they still thought it strange to see one sportsman wishing his rival well—but they didn't know Eric the man....

In the last few moments before the gun as the athletes were warming up, without any warning, a mighty sound filled the enormous arena. The pipes and drums of the Queen's Cameron Highlanders had struck up with "The Campbells are Coming."

The British team organizer, Sir Philip Christison, sensed some despondency among the British supporters and thought some rousing music would cheer them up. Maybe it would spur Eric Liddell too. After all, he was a Scot and the skirl of the pipes would surely send the blood racing through his veins—just at a time when it was most needed.

...Eventually, the music faded. A tense silence returned only to be shattered by the sharp crack of the starting pistol, and Eric was off.

No one could believe what they were seeing. Right from the start he leapt into a three-meter lead. On he went with that awful running style of his. He resembled a feeble swimmer, out of his depth and struggling for air; thrashing out with arms and legs.

Everyone knew he couldn't keep up that pace. A 100-meter man couldn't do what he was doing. Still, he pounded on. Guy Butler was running his heart out too. For a while the crowd seemed hypnotized. Then the unexpected occurred. Fitch, one of the Americans, overtook Butler to sprint closer and closer to Eric who was still in the lead. But again, the unexpected happened. Eric began to run faster.

Closer and closer he drew to the tape—without seeing it. His head was back on his shoulders and his eyes were looking up to heaven. From out of nowhere, it seemed, hosts of British Union Jacks appeared among the onlookers to wave him on to victory.

Suddenly, after what seemed like miles, the 400-meter race was over. Eric Liddell reached the tape a full five meters ahead of Fitch, with the injured Guy Butler sprinting into third place to take a bronze.

The crowd's roar could be heard all over Paris. Then, in a brief spell of quiet, a voice boomed out over the speaker to announce that Eric had run the race in a new world record time of 47.6 seconds. This time it seemed the cheers would be heard across the channel in Britain....

Sir Philip Christison was confident the stirring effect of the pipes and drums had spurred the 22-year-old Scot to victory that day. But Eric knew it was something quite different. It was all due to a few simple words written on a scrap of paper.

In the days leading up to his races, the masseur officially assigned to care for the British team had come to know Eric very well and he liked him immensely.

To try in some way to show the athlete how much he admired him, as Eric was leaving his hotel for the Colombes Stadium, the masseur came up to him and pressed a piece of folded paper into his hand.

Later, in one of the few quiet times of that day, he unfolded the paper and read: "In the old book it says, 'He that honors me I will honor.' Wishing you the best of success always."

For the 1924 Olympic Games a motto had been especially created. It was "Citius, Althius, Fortius," meaning "Faster, Higher, Stronger" and it could apply to no competitor more than to Eric Liddell.

A Candy Bar

Doris Sanford

There was once a lady who worked in a high rise office building in London. Every day for her coffee break she went down to the first floor cafeteria and purchased a Kit Kat candy bar from the vending machine, and a cup of coffee. This day was no different. After finding a small table in the corner and seating herself, she leaned over to search for something in her purse. When she sat up again a gentleman had seated himself across from her at the table. He had a cup of coffee, a doughnut and her Kit Kat bar in his mouth. He didn't apologize or offer any explanation. He simply ate it.

She was surprised and irritated, but said nothing. As quickly as possible she drank her coffee. The more she thought about it, however, the angrier she became. Finally she stood to leave and stomped over beside him, grabbing the remnant of his doughnut and stuffing it in her mouth. As best she could she said, "There now. How does *that* feel?" and marched back to her office, where she again opened her purse. To her horror, there on top was *her* Kit Kat candy bar!

What To Listen For

Tim Hansel

An Indian was in downtown New York, walking along with his friend, who lived in New York City. Suddenly he said, "I hear a cricket."

"Oh, you're crazy," his friend replied.

"No, I hear a cricket. I do! I'm sure of it."

"It's the noon hour. You know there are people bustling around, cars honking, taxis squealing, noises from the city. I'm sure you can't hear it."

"I'm sure I do." He listened attentively and then walked to the corner, across the street, and looked all around. Finally on the other corner he found a shrub in a large cement planter. He dug beneath the leaf and found a cricket.

His friend was duly astounded. But the Indian said, "No, my ears are no different from yours. It simply depends on what you are listening to. Here, let me show you."

He reached into his pocket and pulled out a handful of change—a few quarters, some dimes, nickels, and pennies. And he dropped it on the concrete.

Every head within a block turned.

"You see what I mean?" the Indian said as he began picking up his coins. "It all depends on what you are listening for."

Good Turn

Retold by Nola Bertelson

Eleven-year-old Jeff, along with the rest of the boy scout troop, did a "good turn" in order to complete a project for their next service badge. The boys gathered at Mr. and Mrs. Meyers' house and spent some time cleaning the snow and ice off the older couple's sidewalks and porch.

But somehow, Jeff didn't feel satisfied. To him, it felt sort of phony. He talked it over with his scoutmaster. "I don't think it really helped them much. It seems like we did it more to earn points for ourselves."

"You could go back on your own to see what you can do to help them," the discerning scoutmaster suggested. "And, if you don't tell anyone about it, you won't be earning 'points' in any way."

To Jeff, that sounded like the perfect solution. Several days passed before Jeff worked up enough courage to return to the house. When he finally knocked on the door, he was nervous, but he was determined to follow through with *his* good turn.

It was Mrs. Meyers who opened the door. She listened carefully, and then politely declined Jeff's offer of help. Mr. Meyers, however, overheard the conversation.

"I know something you can help with," he said cheerfully, and he motioned Jeff to follow him into the kitchen. Mr. Meyers had several projects there needing the aid of sturdy arms and legs. Jeff was kept busy carrying items up and down from the basement, and climbing a stepladder to reach high shelves and corners. That evening when he climbed into bed, Jeff felt very tired, but he felt more satisfied with his work than he had after shoveling snow.

After school the next day, Jeff returned to the Meyers'

home. This time they were both willing to accept his help with several tasks.

He stopped by a third time a few days later.

"No work today," Mrs. Meyers said. For a moment Jeff felt offended, but then he saw the twinkle in Mr. Meyers' eyes. "Today we have a surprise for you." With that they ushered him into the small dining room.

A charming table-setting for three sat waiting, complete with lace cloth, flowers, and a silver plate filled with diamond-shaped cookies. Jeff was quite surprised but he remembered his manners and held a chair for Mrs. Meyers as she sat down.

"These are poor man's cookies," Mrs. Meyers said as she passed the silver plate to Jeff.

"Why are they called that?" he asked, thinking it an odd name for cookies.

Mr. Meyers answered, "After you buy all the ingredients, you're a poor man!" Thus began an hour or so of laughter and conversation. As the couple shared pictures and told stories about their family that now lived far away, Jeff's heart was softened as he realized how lonely they were. He decided to stop by often and "help out."

All during the years of junior and senior high, Jeff continued to find reasons to stop by. There was always some way he could pitch in. Between mowing lawns, raking leaves, clearing snow, weeding gardens, and all kinds of indoor projects, the three talked and laughed and grew to be very important in each other's lives.

All too soon the time came when Jeff entered the Army to serve his country. Letters had to replace the face-to-face talks. Every holiday season Jeff looked forward to receiving a package from the Meyerses—always a batch of poor man's cookies.

Mr. Meyers died while Jeff was in the service, and Jeff felt his loss immensely. When he returned home, he picked up his old habit of stopping in "just to help out a bit." He knew Mrs. Meyers was lonelier than ever without Mr. Meyers. And she continued to serve poor man's cookies on the silver platter in the dining room. It was so touching to see her continue to set three places at the table for their special tea times.

Then, Jeff was getting married. Mrs. Meyers would not have missed his wedding for anything. She left her house the day of the ceremony carrying her gift—a "rag" rug that she wove by hand, and a double batch of poor man's cookies. Tucked inside the package was her special cookie recipe. As it turned out, that was the last batch of cookies she made; Mrs. Meyers died a few months later.

For many years, Jeff kept his promise to himself that he would never tell anyone about the "special project" helping the Meyerses. He thought that drawing the attention to himself would spoil the "good turn."

The difference between holding on to a hurt
or releasing it with forgiveness—
is like the difference between laying your
head down at night on a pillow filled with thorns
or a pillow filled with rose petals.

Loren Fischer

Behind the Quick Sketch

Joni Eareckson Tada

My art instructor, an excellent craftsman, told me a compelling story about the benefits of diligent work.

Many years ago there was a famous Japanese artist named Hokusai, whose paintings were coveted by royalty. One day a nobleman requested a special painting of his prized bird. He left the bird with Hokusai, and the artist told the nobleman to return in a week.

The master missed his beautiful bird, and was anxious to return at the end of the week, not only to secure his favorite pet, but his painting as well. When the nobleman arrived, however, the artist humbly requested a two-week postponement.

The two-week delay stretched into two months—and then six.

A year later, the nobleman stormed into Hokusai's studio. He refused to wait any longer and demanded both his bird and his painting. Hokusai, in the Japanese way, bowed to the nobleman, turned to his workshop table, and picked up a brush and a large sheet of rice paper. Within moments he had effortlessly painted an exact likeness of the lovely bird.

The bird's owner was stunned by the painting.

And then he was angry. "Why did you keep me waiting for a year if you could have done the painting in such a short time?"

"You don't understand," Hokusai replied. Then he escorted the nobleman into a room where the walls were covered with paintings of the same bird. None of them, however, matched the grace and beauty of the final rendering....

This must also be true of the canvas of our lives.... If we want to have something of real worth and lasting value in our character, it won't come easy.

It never does.

Androclus and the Lion

Retold by Casandra Lindell
This is based on a true story recorded in Noctes Attica Vol. XV
by Autus Gellius

Heart racing, legs aching, he reached the forest; Androclus knew no other safe place. He could survive there—find roots and berries, avoid wild animals. He had few choices—he would be executed as a runaway slave if caught.

He wondered how it would be, living in terror of discovery. Every pine cone that fell softly to the mossy carpet beneath his feet was enough to make him jump, jerking his head around so wide eyes could search for soldiers.

He needed shelter. Rain was in the air, and it would soon be dark. Through the trees, he saw an opening in the rocks. Thinking it might be big enough to sleep in just for one night, Androclus veered toward it.

Suddenly he stopped. Lying to the right of the opening was a lion. Instinct kicked in and Androclus ran, praying that the creature had already eaten.

Hearing no sound of pursuit, he slowed, and then stopped. Looking back, he saw that the lion had not chased. In fact, its only movement had been to roll its head to look at the man—rather sorrowfully, Androclus thought.

Slowly, he retraced his steps. The lion was in pain. Androclus spoke softly, stroking mane and back, gently searching for injury. Finally, he found it—a nasty gash on the lion's hind leg that had been bleeding for some time and showed no sign of stopping. The man tore cloth from the hem of his tunic and cleaned the wound. The lion shuddered and groaned. Finally, it slept.

Just then the clouds let go of their rain. Androclus crawled into the cave and fell asleep immediately. It had been a long run from the city. Minutes later, he awoke as the lion crawled into the cave next to him, dragging its leg, and collapsed with a wheezing sigh.

The cave was large, and man and beast lived together for several weeks. Androclus found a fresh spring not too far away. The two hunted and gathered the food each needed.

One day, while scooping water from the stream, Androclus felt something sharp press into his neck.

"Don't move," a quarrelsome voice ordered. "There is quite a reward for the life of a runaway slave, you know. Now, stand up slowly."

Forced back to the city, Androclus thought of his friend the lion, knowing they would never meet again. He was taken to stand before the Emperor in court, and was there sentenced to death. Soldiers took him to a stone cell in the halls under the arena until the time of execution.

Finally, they led him into the arena. The crowd spat its hatred. But they began a thunderous cheer when a lion was loosed—a lion that had not been fed for several days, a lion poked and prodded into fierce anger by the soldiers. It roared when it saw the man, and bounded headlong toward its prey.

Androclus knew he didn't stand a chance. Still, his muscles tensed for the fight, readied for pain. How different things had turned out when he befriended a lion in pain instead of poking and prodding one. He closed his eyes, waiting for the weight of the animal, steeling against the first slashing blow.

Instead of searing pain, he felt the tongue of the lion wash his face as it knocked him to the ground. Androclus opened his eyes—face to face with his friend from the forest. Instead of pouncing to kill, even after days of hunger and torment, the lion, once so gently cared for, fawned over the man like a friendly dog.

The crowd was instantly silent, the Emperor stunned. He called Androclus to him, and Androclus told his story.

"Both Androclus and his lion are hereby freed," the Emperor announced. "Such amazing kindness and gratitude between fierce enemies should be greatly rewarded."

MEASURE OF A MAN

The ultimate measure of a man is not where he stands in moments of comfort and convenience, but where he stands at times of challenge and controversy.

Martin Luther King

Gossip

Billy Graham

There is a story of a woman in England who came to her vicar with a troubled conscience. The vicar knew her to be an habitual gossip—she maligned nearly everyone in the village.

"How can I make amends?" she pleaded. The vicar said, "If you want to make peace with your conscience, take a bag of goose feathers and drop one on the porch of each one you have slandered."

When she had done so, she came back to the vicar and said, "Is that all?" "No," said the wise old minister, "you must go now and gather up every feather and bring them all back to me."

After a long time the woman returned without a single feather. "The wind has blown them all away." she said. "My good woman," said the vicar, "so it is with gossip. Unkind words are easily dropped, but we can never take them back again."

The Toe-Tapper

Joan Sparks

One day a wise man came to a small town. He needed a place to stay so he went to the first church he found. Inside, a small group of people argued about how they could best please God.

"I'll help you," the man said, "but you must promise to use what I do to glorify God."

"Oh, we will," the people assured him. "We will."

He gave each of them gifts—one was to be a pianist, another a flutist. To one he gave a cello, to another a violin, and to yet another he gave the role of toe-tapper.

The people worked long and hard to prepare a song of praise for the church. The music became more and more beautiful.

One afternoon during practice the violinist said to the pianist, "I'm so glad I have the important job of playing the violin. I'd sure hate to be only a toe-tapper." The toe-tapper was so hurt that he went home.

The next day, when the group met to practice, nothing came together right. Finally, the flutist said, "Without the toe-tapper here I don't know when to come in for my part." They started over time and time again, but the music sounded terrible.

It was then that the violinist spoke up in a very sad voice. "I'm sorry. This is all my fault. I thought I was so important that I didn't need the help of the toe-tapper. I was wrong!"

So he led the way to the toe-tapper's house and asked him to come back with them. The toe-tapper agreed and once again the music was beautiful.

Then, one Sunday, they played their music in church. God looked down and smiled.

I think he even winked at the toe-tapper.

Taking Sides

Zig Ziglar

A little guy was confronted by three bullies, any one of whom could have obliterated him, and they were giving some evidence that they had that plan in mind. The little guy was very bright, so he backed away from the three bullies, drew a line in the dirt, backed up a few more steps, looked into the eyes of the biggest of the three, and said, "Now, you just step across that line." Confidently, the big bully did exactly that, and the little guy just grinned and said, "Now, we're both on the same side."

The reason a dog has so many friends
is because he wags his tail instead of his tongue.

The Dress

Margaret Jensen

Mary was young, filled with dreams of love for God and His service. John, restless and impatient in his new pastorate in the farmlands of Wisconsin, longed for the libraries and action of New York City or Chicago, where he had attended seminary. John's brilliant mind craved books. Mary saw beauty in everything—the smell of the freshly plowed fields, the song of a bird, the first signs of spring, crocuses and violets. Mary sang to the wind and laughed with the birds. But she had one secret longing, a new dress for spring. Not the somber brown or black, befitting a minister's wife, but a soft voile, billowing dress with lace around the neck and sleeves and a big sash.

There was no money! Carefully she laid plans. She would put pennies into a box until there was enough money to buy a new kerosene lamp for John and material for a new dress. She would reuse the lace from an old velvet dress in the trunk. Someday she would make a blue velvet dress for her baby Louise.

The day came when the treadle machine purred like music while Mary sang and sewed. Golden-haired Louise played with empty spools and clothes pins. The small house shone clean. The new lamp had a place of honor on John's reading table.

In a playful mood, Mary pulled down her long brown hair, brushed it in the morning sun. Then she put on her new dress, soft pink voile with violets and lace. A sash tied at the back, and Mary swung around to the delightful squeals of Louise. It was spring! She was young, just 23, with another new life within her and Louise to rock and love. The wilderness church, the somber immigrants tilling the land, and the severe harshness of long winter had isolated the young wife into her world of poetry and song. But she had grown to love the faithful people and shared their joys and sorrows. Today, she danced with abandoned joy in her new billowing dress.

With the flash of summer lightning, Mary was whirled around by an angry John, whose storm of frustration unleashed the fury within him. "Money for foolishness! No libraries, no books—no one to talk to about anything except cows and chickens, planting and harvest."

Like a smoldering volcano, John erupted with rage and ripped the dress to shreds. Just as suddenly the storm was over, and the galloping hoofs of John's horse broke the quiet terror. As he rode into the wind, he unleashed the remainder of his fury on the passing fields and their wide-eyed cows and clucking chickens. He longed to gallop from Wisconsin to the heart of New York—his beloved library.

Huddled in a corner, Mary clutched Louise and the shredded dress. Trembling with fear and anger she remained motionless. Too drained to weep, she was sick with an emptiness and an unutterable longing for her mother. There was no one to turn to in the lonely farmland. She remembered Psalm 34:4. "I sought the Lord, and He heard me, and delivered me from all my fears." Then she wept, long and deep, and cried unto the Lord.

Mary set her heart to seek a way of escape. She would make a pallet up in the loft and take Louise to sleep with her. John would sleep alone. Then she folded the shredded dress in a small package and hid it in her trunk. Pastor Hansen was coming to visit the near churches and Mary decided to bide her time, to quietly wait and show the dress to Pastor Hansen, then ask for assistance to leave John and return to her mother. With quiet determination she put on her dark dress and combed her hair into a severe knot, befitting a minister's wife. She set the table for supper. When John returned late in the night his supper was in the warming oven. Mary was asleep in the loft with Louise curled in her arms.

Quietly John ate his supper and looked for Mary. When he found her in the loft, he ordered her back to their bed and put Louise in her crib. Mary gently tucked Louise in her crib and obediently went to bed. John's storm had passed, but he was unaware of the debris in its wake.

Life went on as usual, but the song was gone and Mary's steps were weighted with bitterness. She quietly waited and thought out her plans.

The arrival of Pastor Hansen brought a new exuberance to John as the two ministers discussed books and theology and the work of the church conference. Mary served quietly. No one would have guessed the anguish behind her gentle face as she worshipped with the faithful congregations, but heard little of the sermons.

The final service was drawing to a close and, as yet, Mary had not had the opportunity to see Pastor Hansen alone. She had to find the opening, perhaps this Sunday afternoon, when John would visit a shut-in member while Pastor Hansen would meditate on the evening message. With a quickened mind she decided to listen to the sermon and perhaps use his comments as an opening.

"The text this morning is found in Mark 11:25 (KJV). 'When ye stand praying, forgive.' Forgiveness is not optional, but a definite act of the will to forgive, in obedience to God's command. The feeling comes later, the feeling of peace. When we offer to God our hurts and despair, God will pour His love and compassion into the wounds, and His healing will come."

Oh, no, Mary cried inside. I can't forgive, and I can never forget.

The sermon continued, "Someone may be thinking, I can never forget, even if I could forgive. You are right, you can't forget, but you needn't be devastated by the remembering. God's love and His forgiveness can and will cushion the memory until the imprint is gone. When you forgive you must destroy the evidence, and remember only to love."

John and Pastor Hansen rode home with Deacon Olsen. Mary stepped into her buggy, tied her wide black hat with a scarf and carefully secured Louise around her waist. As the horse, Dolly, trotted briskly down the country road, Mary's scalding tears poured forth.

She knew what she must do. She would obey God. Without waiting to unhitch Dolly, she fled from the buggy and placed Louise in her crib. With trembling hands, Mary took out of the trunk the package with the torn dress, but she couldn't let go.

The Sunday dinner was in the warming oven; Mary poked the fire and added more wood. Automatically she put on the coffee pot and set the table. "The evidence must go," rang in her memory. "I forgive you, John." She finally picked up the tattered dress with one hand and the stove lid with the other. Tears splashed on the fire as she watched the dress burn slowly.

"True forgiveness destroys the evidence," pounded so loudly in her heart that she failed to hear John's footsteps. "Mary, what are you doing?" Trembling with sobs, she said, "I am destroying the evidence."

To herself she said, "My offering to God."

Then John remembered! Pale and shaken he murmured, "Please forgive me."

Fifty-eight years later, when John had gone home to the Lord and she missed him terribly, Mary had a dream. Three angels appeared to her and said, "Come, we are going to a celebration." Over the arm of one angel was draped a beautiful dress.

Distant Relatives

Carla Muir

A certain old recluse lived deep in the mountains of Colorado. When he died, distant relatives came from the city to collect his valuables. Upon arriving, all they saw was an old shack with an outhouse beside it. Inside the shack, next to the rock fireplace, was an old cooking pot and his mining equipment. A cracked table with a three-legged chair stood guard by a tiny window, and a kerosene lamp served as the centerpiece for the table. In a dark corner of the little room was a dilapidated cot with a threadbare bedroll on it.

They picked up some of the old relics and started to leave. As they were driving away, an old friend of the recluse, on his mule, flagged them down. "Do you mind if I help myself to what's left in my friend's cabin?" he asked. "Go right ahead," they replied. After all, they thought, what inside that shack could be worth anything?

The old friend entered the shack and walked directly over to the table. He reached under it and lifted one of the floor boards. He then proceeded to take out all the gold his friend had discovered over the past 53 years—enough to have built a palace. The recluse died with only his friend knowing his true worth. As the friend looked out of the little window and watched the cloud of dust behind the relative's car disappear, he said, "They shoulda got to know him better."

It's More Than a Job

Charles Swindoll

A young fella rushed into a service station and asked the manager if he had a pay phone. The manager nodded, "Sure, over there." The boy pushed in a couple of coins, dialed, and waited for an answer. Finally, someone came on the line. "Uh, sir," he said in a deep voice, "could you use an honest, hardworking young man to work for you?" The station manager couldn't help overhearing the question. After a moment or two the boy said, "Oh, you already have an honest, hardworking young man? Well, okay. Thanks just the same."

With a broad smile stretched across his face, he hung up the phone and started back to his car, humming and obviously elated. "Hey, just a minute!" the station manager called after him. "I couldn't help but hear your conversation. Why are you so happy? I thought the guy said he already had somebody and didn't need you?" The young man smiled. "Well, you see, I am the honest, hardworking young man. I was just checking up on my job!"

A *Tender Warrior*

Stu Weber

What does a healthy man look like? I can't help but recall a statement from a young man who lives near us—a sixteen-year-old high school sophomore. His parents divorced when he was eight years old. His father left and has never returned. His stepdad, a tyrannical and poor excuse for a man, treats him poorly. Tells him to "shut up" all the time. Tells him he's worthless, stupid, and will never amount to anything.

But just ask the boy about his dream and his eyes will light up. This is what he'll tell you: "I'd like to find out where my real dad lives. And I'd like to move in next door without him knowing who I was. And—I'd like to just become his friend. Once I had become his friend, then maybe it would be OK for me to move on."

This same young man who has had all kinds of difficulty in his life was asked to write an essay on the subject, "What is a man?" The following is his brief essay—written by a boy who has never really been around a man, never really seen one. But I think there is something so inherent, so ingrained, so intrinsic, so fundamental, that even a young boy who has never seen it modeled can put it into words. Here's what he wrote:

A real man is kind.

A real man is caring.

A real man walks away from silly macho fights.

A real man helps his wife.

A real man helps his kids when they are sick.

A real man doesn't run from his problems.

A real man sticks to his word and keeps his promises.

A real man is honest.

A real man is not in trouble with the law.

It's one lonely boy's vision of a man who stays. A man who is both an authority and under authority.

It's a vision of a Tender Warrior.

Character is what you are in the dark.

Dwight L. Moody

Love

ONENESS

*Henceforth there will be such
a oneness between us—
that when one weeps
the other will taste salt.*

Author Unknown

The Pencil Box

Doris Sanford

I was deep in thought at my office, preparing a lecture to be given that evening at a college across town, when the phone rang. A woman I had never met introduced herself and said that she was the mother of a seven-year-old and that she was dying. She said that her therapist had advised her that discussing her pending death with her son would be too traumatic for him, but somehow that didn't feel right to her.

Knowing that I worked with grieving children, she asked my advice. I told her that our heart is often smarter than our brain and that I thought she knew what would be best for her son. I also invited her to attend the lecture that night since I was speaking about how children cope with death. She said she would be there.

I wondered later if I would recognize her at the lecture, but my question was answered when I saw a frail woman being half carried into the room by two adults. I talked about the fact that children usually sense the truth long before they are told and that they often wait until they feel adults are ready to talk about it before sharing their concerns and questions. I said that children usually can handle truth better than denial, even though the denial is intended to protect them from pain. I said that respecting children meant including them in the family sadness, not shutting them out.

She had heard enough. At the break, she hobbled to the podium and through her tears she said, "I knew it in my heart. I just knew I should tell him." She said that she would tell him that night.

The next morning I received another phone call from her.

She could hardly talk but I managed to hear the story through her choked voice. She awakened him when they got home the night before and quietly said, "Derek, I have something to tell you." He quickly interrupted her saying, "Oh, Mommy, is it now that you are going to tell me that you are dying?" She held him close and they both sobbed while she said, "Yes."

After a few minutes the little boy wanted down. He said that he had something for her that he had been saving. In the back of one of his drawers was a dirty pencil box. Inside the box was a letter written in simple scrawl. It said, "Good-bye, Mom. I will always love you."

How long he had been waiting to hear the truth, I don't know. I do know that two days later Mom died. In her casket was placed a dirty pencil box and a letter.

Measure wealth not by the things you have,
but by the things you have for which you
would not take money.

Anonymous

She's My Precious

Robertson McQuilkin
(condensed)

Written six years after stepping down as president of Columbia Bible College and Seminary to care for his wife, Muriel, who suffers from Alzheimer's.

Seventeen summers ago, Muriel and I began our journey into the twilight. It's midnight now, at least for her, and sometimes I wonder when dawn will break. Even the dread of Alzheimer's disease isn't supposed to attack so early and torment so long. Yet, in her silent world, Muriel is so content, so lovable. If Jesus took her home, how I would miss her gentle, sweet presence. Yes, there are times when I get irritated, but not often. It doesn't make much sense to get angry. And besides, perhaps the Lord has been answering the prayer of my youth to mellow my spirit.

Once, though, I completely lost it. In the days when Muriel could still stand and walk and we had not resorted to diapers, sometimes there were "accidents." I was on my knees beside her, trying to clean up the mess as she stood, confused, by the toilet. It would have been easier if she weren't so insistent on helping. I got more and more frustrated. Suddenly, to make her stand still, I slapped her calf—as if that would do any good. It wasn't a hard slap, but she was startled. I was, too. Never in our forty-four years of marriage had I ever so much as touched her in anger or in rebuke of any kind. Never; wasn't even tempted, in fact. But, now, when she needed me most....

Sobbing, I pled with her to forgive me—no matter that she didn't understand words any better than she could speak them. So I turned to the Lord to tell Him how sorry I was. It took me days to get over it. Maybe God bottled those tears to quench the fires that might ignite again some day.

Recently, a student wife asked me, "Don't you ever get tired?"

"Tired? Every night. That's why I go to bed."

"No, I mean tired of..." and she tilted her head toward Muriel, who sat silently in her wheelchair, her vacant eyes saying, "No one at home just now." I responded to Cindi's question, "Why no, I don't get tired. I love to care for her. She's my precious...."

Love is said to evaporate if the relationship is not mutual, if it's not physical, if the other person doesn't communicate, or if one party doesn't carry his or her share of the load. When I hear the litany of essentials for a happy marriage, I count off what my beloved can no longer contribute, and then I contemplate how truly mysterious love is.

What some people find so hard to understand is that loving Muriel isn't hard. They wonder about my former loves—like my work. "Do you miss being president?" a student asked as we sat in our little garden. I told him I'd never thought about it, but, on reflection, no. As exhilarating as my work had been, I enjoyed learning to cook and keep house. No, I'd never looked back.

But that night I did reflect on his question and turned it to the Lord. "Father, I like this assignment, and I have no regrets. But if a coach puts a man on the bench, he must not want him in the game. You needn't tell me, of course, but I'd like to know—why didn't you keep me in the game?"

I didn't sleep well that night and awoke contemplating the puzzle. Muriel was still mobile at that time, so we set out on our morning walk around the block. She wasn't too sure on her feet, so we went slowly and held hands as we always do. This day I heard footsteps behind me and looked back to see the familiar form of a local derelict behind us. He staggered past us, then turned and looked us up and down. "Tha's good. I like 'at," he said. "Tha's real good. I likes it." He turned and headed back down the street, mumbling to himself over and over, "Tha's good. I likes it."

When Muriel and I reached our little garden and sat down, his words came back to me. Then the realization hit me; the Lord had spoken through an inebriated old derelict. "It is you who is whispering to my spirit, 'I likes it, tha's good,'" I said aloud. "I may be on the bench, but if you like it and say it's good, that's all that counts...."

I think my life is happier than the lives of 95 percent of the people on planet Earth.

The Final Bid

Robert Strand

The very wealthy English Baron Fitzgerald had only one child, a son, who understandably was the apple of his eye, the center of his affections, an only child, the focus of this little family's attention.

The son grew up, but in his early teens his mother died, leaving him and his father. Fitzgerald grieved over the loss of his wife but devoted himself to fathering their son. In the passing of time, the son became very ill and died in his late teens. In the meantime, the Fitzgerald financial holdings greatly increased. The father had used much of his wealth to acquire art works of the "masters."

And with the passing of more time, Fitzgerald himself became ill and died. Previous to his death he had carefully prepared his will with explicit instructions as to how his estate would be settled. He had directed that there would be an auction in which his entire collection of art would be sold. Because of the quantity and quality of the art works in his collection which was valued in the millions of English pounds, a huge crowd of prospective buyers gathered, expectantly. Among them were many museum curators and private collectors eager to bid.

The art works were displayed for viewing before the auction began. Among them was one painting which received little attention. It was of poor quality and done by an unknown local artist. It happened to be a portrait of Fitzgerald's only son.

When the time came for the auction to begin, the auctioneer gaveled the crowd to attention and before the bidding began, the attorney read first from the will of Fitzgerald which instructed that the first painting to be auctioned was the painting of "my beloved son."

The poor quality painting didn't receive any bidders...except one! The only bidder was the old servant who had known the son and loved him and served him and for sentimental reasons offered the only bid. For less than an English pound he bought the painting.

The auctioneer stopped the bidding and asked the attorney to read again from the will. The crowd was hushed, it was quite unusual, and the attorney read from the Fitzgerald will: "Whoever buys the painting of my son gets all my art collection. The auction is over!"

The first duty of love is to listen.

Paul Tillich

Shoooooppping!!

Gary Smalley

A fter a tearful session with my wife, I decided to commit myself wholeheartedly to understanding and relating to her. But I didn't know where to start.

Suddenly, I had an idea that I knew would get me nominated for Husband of the Year. I could do something adventurous with Norma—like going shopping! Of course! My wife loves to shop. Since I had never volunteered to go with her before, this would demonstrate how much I really cared. I could arrange for a baby-sitter and then take her to one of her favorite places in the world: the mall!

I'm not sure what emotional and physiological changes ignite inside my wife upon hearing the words "the mall," but when I told her my idea, it was obvious something dramatic was happening. Her eyes lit up like a Christmas tree, and she trembled with excitement—the same reaction I'd had when someone gave me two tickets to an NFL play-off game.

That next Saturday afternoon, when Norma and I went shopping together, I ran face first into a major barrier that bars many men and women from meaningful communication. What I discovered blew open the door to understanding and relating to Norma.... Here's what happened:

As we drove up to the mall, Norma told me she needed to look for a new blouse. So after we parked the car and walked into the nearest clothing store, she held up a blouse and asked, "What do you think?"

"Great," I said. "Let's get it." But really, I was thinking, *Great! If she hurries up and gets this blouse, we will be back home in plenty of time to watch the college game on TV.*

Then she picked up another blouse and said, "What do you think about this one?"

"It's great, too!" I said. "Get either one. No, get both!"

But after looking at a number of blouses on the rack, we walked out of the store empty-handed. Then we went into another store, and she did the same thing. And then into another store. And another. And another!

As we went in and out of all the shops, I became increasingly anxious. The thought even struck me, not only will I miss the half-time highlights, but I will also miss the entire game!

After looking at what seemed like hundreds of blouses, I could tell I was beginning to lose it. At the rate we were going, I would miss the entire season! And that's when it happened.

Instead of picking up a blouse at the next store we entered, she held up a dress that was our daughter's size. "What do you think about this for Kari?" she asked.

Taxed beyond any mortal's limits, my willpower cracked, and I blurted out, "What do you mean, 'What do I think about a dress for Kari?' We're here shopping for blouses for you, not dresses for Kari!"

As if that wasn't bad enough, we left that store without buying anything, and then she asked if we could stop and have coffee! We'd already been at the mall for sixty-seven entire minutes, which beat my previous endurance record by *half an hour.* I couldn't *believe* it—she actually had the nerve to want to sit around and discuss the kids' lives!

That night, I began to understand a common difference between men and women. I was shopping for blouses...I was *hunting* for blouses! I wanted to conquer the blouse, bag it, and then get back home where important things were, like my Saturday-afternoon football game!

My wife, however, looked at shopping from opposite extremes. For her, it meant more than simply buying a blouse.

It was a way to spend time talking together as we enjoyed several hours away from the children and Saturday afternoon football.

Like most men, I thought a trip to the mall meant going shopping. But to my wife it meant *shoooopppping!*

A successful marriage requires falling in love many times, always with the same person.

Mignon McLaughlin

Heirloom

Ann Weems
Retold by Alice Gray

It had belonged to Great-grandmother and he knew he must be very careful. The vase was one of mother's dearest treasures. She had told him so.

The vase, placed high on the mantle, was out of the reach of little hands, but somehow he managed. He just wanted to see if the tiny little rosebud border went all around the back. He didn't realize that a boy's five-year-old hands are sometimes clumsy and not meant to hold delicate porcelain treasures. It shattered when it hit the floor, and he began to cry. That cry soon became a sobbing wail, growing louder and louder. From the kitchen his mother heard her son crying and she came running. Her footsteps hurried down the hall and came around the corner. She stopped then, looked at him, and saw what he had done.

Between his sobs, he could hardly speak the words, "I broke…the vase."

And then his mother gave him a gift.

With a look of relief, his mother said "Oh, thank heavens, I thought you were hurt!" And then she held him tenderly until his sobbing stopped.

She made it very clear—he was the treasure. Though now a grown man, it is a gift he still carries in his heart.

It Happened on the Brooklyn Subway

Paul Deutschman

The car was crowded, and there seemed to be no chance of a seat. But as I entered, a man sitting by the door suddenly jumped up to leave, and I slipped into the empty seat.

I've been living in New York long enough not to start conversations with strangers. But, being a photographer, I have the peculiar habit of analyzing people's faces, and I was struck by the features of the passenger on my left. He was probably in his late 30s, and when he glanced up, his eyes seemed to have a hurt expression in them. He was reading a Hungarian-language newspaper, and something prompted me to say in Hungarian, "I hope you don't mind if I glance at your paper."

The man seemed surprised to be addressed in his native language. But he only answered politely, "You may read it now. I'll have time later on."

During the half-hour ride to town, we had quite a conversation. He said his name was Bela Paskin. A law student when World War II started, he had been put into a German labor battalion and sent to the Ukraine. Later he was captured by the Russians and put to work burying the German dead. After the war, he covered hundreds of miles on foot until he reached his home in Debrecen, a large city in eastern Hungary.

I myself knew Debrecen quite well, and we talked about it for a while. Then he told me the rest of his story. When he went to the apartment once occupied by his father, mother, brothers, and sisters, he found strangers living there. Then he went upstairs to the apartment that he and his wife once had. It was also occupied by strangers. None of them had ever heard of his family.

As he was leaving, full of sadness, a boy ran after him, calling, "Paskin bacsi! Paskin bacsi!" That means "Uncle Paskin." The child was the son of some old neighbors of his. He went to the boy's home and talked to his parents. "Your whole family is dead," they told him. "The Nazis took them and your wife to Auschwitz,"

Auschwitz was one of the worst Nazi concentration camps. Paskin gave up all hope. A few days later, too heartsick to remain any longer in Hungary, he set out on foot again, stealing across border after border until he reached Paris. He managed to immigrate to the United States in October 1947, just three months before I met him.

All the time he had been talking, I kept thinking that somehow his story seemed familiar. A young woman whom I met recently at the home of friends had also been from Debrecen; she had been sent to Auschwitz; from there she had been transferred to work in a German munitions factory. Her relatives had been killed in the gas chambers. Later, she was liberated by the Americans and was brought here in the first boatload of displaced persons in 1946.

Her story had moved me so much that I had written down her address and phone number, intending to invite her to meet my family and thus help relieve the terrible emptiness in her life.

It seemed impossible that there could be any connection between these two people, but as I neared my station, I fumbled anxiously in my address book. I asked in what I hoped was a casual voice, "Was your wife's name Marya?"

He turned pale. "Yes!" he answered. "How did you know?"

He looked as if he were about to faint.

I said, "Let's get off the train." I took him by the arm at the next station and led him to a phone booth. He stood there like a man in a trance while I dialed her phone number.

It seemed hours before Marya Paskin answered. Later I learned her room was alongside the telephone, but she was in the habit of never answering it because she had so few friends and the calls were always for someone else. This time, however, there was no one else at home and, after letting it ring for a while, she responded.

When I heard her voice at last, I told her who I was and asked her to describe her husband. She seemed surprised at the question, but gave me a description. Then I asked her where she had lived in Debrecen, and she told me the address.

Asking her to hold the line, I turned to Paskin and said, "Did you and your wife live on such-and-such a street?"

"Yes!" Bela exclaimed. He was white as a sheet and trembling.

"Try to be calm," I urged him. "Something miraculous is about to happen to you. Here, take this telephone and talk to your wife!"

He nodded his head in mute bewilderment, his eyes bright with tears. He took the receiver, listened a moment to his wife's voice, then cried suddenly, "This is Bela! This is Bela!" and he began to mumble hysterically. Seeing that the poor fellow was so excited he couldn't talk coherently, I took the receiver from his shaking hands.

"Stay where you are," I told Marya, who also sounded hysterical. "I am sending your husband to you. We will be there in a few minutes."

Bela was crying like a baby and saying over and over again, "It is my wife. I go to my wife!"

At first I thought I had better accompany Paskin, lest the man should faint from excitement, but I decided that this was a moment in which no strangers should intrude. Putting Paskin into a taxicab, I directed the driver to take him to Marya's address, paid the fare, and said good-bye.

Bela Paskin's reunion with his wife was a moment so poignant, so electric with suddenly released emotion, that afterward neither he nor Marya could recall much about it.

"I remember only that when I left the phone, I walked to the mirror like in a dream to see if maybe my hair had turned gray," she said later. "The next thing I know, a taxi stops in front of the house, and it is my husband who comes toward me. Details I cannot remember; only this I know—that I was happy for the first time in many years....

"Even now it is difficult to believe that it happened. We have both suffered so much; I have almost lost the capability to not be afraid. Each time my husband goes from the house, I say to myself, 'Will anything happen to take him from me again?'"

Her husband is confident that no horrible misfortune will ever befall them. "Providence has brought us together," he says simply. "It was meant to be."

Love is a Grandparent

Erma Bombeck

A preschooler who lives down the street was curious about grandparents. It occurred to me that, to a child, grandparents appear like an apparition with no explanation, no job description and few credentials. They just seem to go with the territory.

This, then, is for the little folks who wonder what a grandparent is.

A grandparent can always be counted on to buy all your cookies, flower seeds, all-purpose greeting cards, transparent tape, paring knives, peanut brittle and ten chances on a pony. (Also a box of taffy when they have dentures.)

A grandparent helps you with the dishes when it is your night.

A grandparent is the only baby-sitter who doesn't charge more after midnight—or anything before midnight.

A grandparent buys you gifts your mother says you don't need.

A grandparent arrives three hours early for your baptism, your graduation and your wedding because he or she wants a seat where he or she can see everything.

A grandparent loves you from when you're a bald baby to a bald father and all the hair in between.

A grandparent will put a sweater on you when she is cold, feed you when she is hungry and put you to bed when she is tired.

A grandparent will brag on you when you get a typing pin that 80 other girls got.

A grandparent will frame a picture of your hand that you traced and put it in her Mediterranean living room.

A grandparent will slip you money just before Mother's Day.

A grandparent will help you with your buttons, your zippers and your shoelaces and not be in any hurry for you to grow up.

When you're a baby, a grandparent will check to see if you are crying when you are sound asleep.

When a grandchild says, "Grandma, how come you didn't have any children?" a grandparent holds back the tears.

Love from the Heart

Chad Miller

Love affairs are not unusual for young teenagers today. It's not particularly surprising when such love affairs are broken for some reason or another. Normally, teens get over the hurt they feel for a broken relationship and discover that there are other "fish in the sea."

This very typical pattern of teen love began as Felipe Garza Jr. began dating Donna Ashlock. Felipe and Donna dated until Donna cooled the romance and began dating other boys.

One day, Donna doubled over in pain. Doctors soon discovered that Donna was dying of a degenerative heart disease and desperately needed a heart transplant. Felipe heard about Donna's condition and told his mother, "I'm going to die and I'm going to give my heart to my girlfriend." Boys say some irrational things like this from time to time. After all, Felipe appeared to his mom to be in perfect health.

Three weeks later, Felipe woke up and complained of pain on the left side of his head. He began losing his breath and couldn't walk. He was taken to the hospital where it was discovered that a blood vessel in his brain had burst and left him brain dead. Felipe's sudden death mystified his doctors! While he remained on a respirator, his family decided to let physicians remove his heart for Donna and his kidneys and eyes for others in need of those organs.

Donna received Felipe's heart! After the transplant, Donna's father told her that Felipe had evidently been sick for about three months before he died. He said, "He donated his kidneys and eyes." There was a pause and Donna said, "And I have his heart."

Her father said, "Yes, that was what he and his family wished." Her expression changed just a little. She then asked her father who knew. He told her, "Everybody." Nothing else was said.

Several days later, a funeral procession seemed to roll on forever through the orchards and fields of Patterson, California. The procession was so long it might have been that of a prince, but it was Felipe. His only claim to fame was his love and his heart. It's unforgettable when a person gives up his life so that someone he loved could live. It would be unforgettable if you had received a new and healthy heart from someone who loved you more than you could appreciate. Every moment you lived would be a tribute to the one who loved you so much that he gave his life for you....

Extraordinary People

Jo Ann Larsen

L arry and Jo Ann were an ordinary couple. They lived in an ordinary house on an ordinary street. Like other ordinary couples, they struggle to make ends meet and to do the right things for their children.

They were ordinary in yet another way; they had their squabbles. Much of their conversation concerned what was wrong in their marriage and who was to blame.

Until one day, when the most extraordinary event took place.

"You know, Jo Ann, I've got a magic chest of drawers. Every time I open them, they're full of socks and underwear," Larry said. "I want to thank you for filling them all these years."

Jo Ann stared at her husband over the top of her spectacles. "What do you want, Larry?"

"Nothing. I just want you to know I appreciate those magic drawers."

This wasn't the first time Larry had done something odd, so Jo Ann pushed the incident out of her mind until a few days later.

"Jo Ann, thank you for recording so many correct check numbers in the ledger this month. You put down the right number fifteen out of sixteen times. That's a record."

Disbelieving what she heard, Jo Ann looked up from her mending: "Larry, you're always complaining about my recording the wrong check numbers. Why stop now?"

"No reason. I just wanted you to know I appreciate the effort you're making."

Jo Ann shook her head and went back to her mending. "What's gotten into him?" she mumbled.

Nevertheless, the next day when Jo Ann wrote a check at the grocery store, she glanced at her checkbook to confirm that she had put down the right check number. "Why do I suddenly care about those dumb numbers?" she asked herself.

She tried to disregard the incident, but Larry's strange behavior intensified.

"Jo Ann, that was a great dinner," he said one evening. "I appreciate all your effort. Why, in the past fifteen years I'll bet you've fixed over 14,000 meals for me and the kids."

"Gee, Jo Ann, the house looks spiffy. You've really worked hard to get it looking so good." And even, "Thanks, Jo Ann, for just being you. I really enjoy your company."

Jo Ann was growing worried. "Where's the sarcasm, the criticism?" she wondered.

Her fears that something peculiar was happening to her husband were confirmed by 16-year-old Shelly, who complained, "Dad's gone bonkers, Mom. He just told me I looked nice. With all this makeup and these sloppy clothes, he still said it. That's not Dad, Mom. What's wrong with him?"

Whatever was wrong, Larry didn't get over it. Day in and day out he continued focusing on the positive. Over the weeks, Jo Ann grew more used to her mate's unusual behavior, and occasionally even gave him a grudging "thank you." She prided herself in taking it all in stride, until one day something so peculiar happened she became completely discombobulated:

"I want you to take a break," Larry said. "I am going to do the dishes. So please take your hands off that frying pan and leave the kitchen."

(Long, long pause.) "Thank you, Larry. Thank you very much!"

Jo Ann's step was now a little lighter, her self-confidence higher, and once in a while she hummed. She didn't seem to experience blue moods much anymore. "I rather like Larry's new behavior," she thought.

That would have been the end of the story except one day, another most extraordinary event took place. This time it was Jo Ann who spoke.

"Larry," she said, "I want to thank you for going to work and providing for us all these years. I don't think I've ever told you how much I appreciate it."

Larry has never revealed the reason for his dramatic change of behavior no matter how hard Jo Ann has pushed for an answer, and so it will likely remain one of life's mysteries. But it's one I'm thankful to live with.

You see, I am Jo Ann.

50 Promises for Marriage

Steve Stephens

1. Start each day with a kiss. 2. Wear your wedding ring at all times. 3. Date once a week. 4. Accept differences. 5. Be polite. 6. Be gentle. 7. Give gifts. 8. Smile often. 9. Touch. 10. Talk about dreams. 11. Select a song that can be "our song." 12. Give back rubs. 13. Laugh together. 14. Send a card for no reason. 15. Do what the other person wants before he or she asks. 16. Listen. 17. Encourage. 18. Do it his or her way. 19. Know his or her needs. 20. Fix the other person's breakfast. 21. Compliment twice a day. 22. Call during the day. 23. Slow down. 24. Hold hands. 25. Cuddle. 26. Ask for each other's opinion. 27. Show respect. 28. Welcome the other person home. 29. Look your best. 30. Wink at each other. 31. Celebrate birthdays in a big way. 32. Apologize. 33. Forgive. 34. Set up a romantic getaway. 35. Ask, "What can I do to make you happier?" 36. Be positive. 37. Be kind. 38. Be vulnerable. 39. Respond quickly to the other person's requests. 40. Talk about your love. 41. Reminisce about your favorite times together. 42. Treat each other's friends and relatives with courtesy. 43. Send flowers every Valentine's Day and anniversary. 44. Admit when wrong. 45. Be sensitive to each other's sexual desires. 46. Pray for each other daily. 47. Watch sunsets together. 48. Say "I love you" frequently. 49. End the day with a hug. 50. Seek outside help when needed.

The Treasure

Alice Gray

The cheerful girl with bouncy golden curls was almost five. Waiting with her mother at the checkout stand, she saw them: a circle of glistening white pearls in a pink foil box.

"Oh please, Mommy. Can I have them? Please, Mommy, please!"

Quickly the mother checked the back of the little foil box and then looked back into the pleading blue eyes of her little girl's upturned face.

"A dollar ninety-five. That's almost $2. If you really want them, I'll think of some extra chores for you and in no time you can save enough money to buy them for yourself. Your birthday's only a week away and you might get another crisp dollar bill from Grandma."

As soon as Jenny got home, she emptied her penny bank and counted out 17 pennies. After dinner, she did more than her share of chores and she went to the neighbor and asked Mrs. McJames if she could pick dandelions for ten cents. On her birthday, Grandma did give her another new dollar bill and at last she had enough money to buy the necklace.

Jenny loved her pearls. They made her feel dressed up and grown up. She wore them everywhere—Sunday school, kindergarten, even to bed. The only time she took them off was when she went swimming or had a bubble bath. Mother said if they got wet, they might turn her neck green.

Jenny had a very loving daddy and every night when she was ready for bed, he would stop whatever he was doing and come upstairs to read her a story. One night when he finished the story, he asked Jenny, "Do you love me?"

"Oh, yes, Daddy. You know that I love you."

"Then give me your pearls."

"Oh, Daddy, not my pearls. But you can have Princess—the white horse from my collection. The one with the pink tail. Remember, Daddy? The one you gave me. She's my favorite."

"That's okay, Honey. Daddy loves you. Good night." And he brushed her cheek with a kiss.

About a week later, after the story time, Jenny's daddy asked again, "Do you love me?"

"Daddy, you know I love you."

"Then give me your pearls."

"Oh, Daddy, not my pearls. But you can have my baby doll. The brand new one I got for my birthday. She is so beautiful and you can have the yellow blanket that matches her sleeper."

"That's okay. Sleep well. God bless you, little one. Daddy loves you." And as always, he brushed her cheek with a gentle kiss.

A few nights later when her daddy came in, Jenny was sitting on her bed with her legs crossed Indian-style. As he came close, he noticed her chin was trembling and one silent tear rolled down her cheek.

"What is it, Jenny? What's the matter?"

Jenny didn't say anything but lifted her little hand up to her daddy. And when she opened it, there was her little pearl necklace. With a little quiver, she finally said, "Here, Daddy. It's for you."

With tears gathering in his own eyes, Jenny's kind daddy reached out with one hand to take the dime-store necklace, and with the other hand he reached into his pocket and pulled out a blue velvet case with a strand of genuine pearls and gave them to Jenny. He had had them all the time. He was just waiting for her to give up the dime-store stuff so he could give her genuine treasure.

So like our heavenly Father.

That Little China Chip

Bettie B. Youngs

One day when I was about nine years old, my mother took a trip into town and put me in charge of my brothers and sisters. As she drove away, I ran into her bedroom and opened the dresser to snoop.

There in the top drawer, beneath soft, wonderful-smelling grown-up garments, was a small wooden jewelry box. I was fascinated by its treasures—the ruby ring left to my mother by her favorite aunt; pearl earrings that once belonged to my grandmother; my mother's own wedding band, which she took off to do farm chores alongside my father.

I tried them all on, filling my mind with glorious images of what it must be like to be a beautiful woman like my mother and to own such exquisite things.

Then I saw there was something tucked behind the piece of red felt lining the lid. Lifting the cloth, I found a little white chip of china.

I picked it up. Why in the world did my mother keep this broken thing? Glinting slightly in the light, it offered no answers.

Some months later, I was setting the dinner table when our neighbor Marge knocked at the door. Mom, busy at the stove, called to her to come in. Glancing at the table, Marge said, "Oh, you're expecting company. I'll stop by another time."

"No, come on in," Mom replied. "We're not expecting anyone."

"But isn't that your good china?" Marge asked. "I'd never trust kids to handle my good dishes!"

Mom laughed. "Tonight's my family's favorite meal. If you set your best table for a special meal with special guests, why not for your family?"

"But your beautiful china!" responded Marge.

"Oh, well," said Mom, "a few broken plates are a small price to pay for the joy we get using them." Then she added, "Besides, every chip and crack has a story to tell."

Reaching into the cupboard, Mom pulled out an old, pieced-together plate. "This one shattered the day we brought Mark home from the hospital," she said. "What a cold and blustery afternoon that was! Judy was only six, but she wanted to be helpful. She dropped the plate carrying it to the sink.

"At first I was upset, but then I told myself, 'I won't let a broken plate change the happiness we feel welcoming our new baby.' Besides, we all had a lot of fun gluing it together!"

Marge looked doubtful.

Mom went to the cupboard again and took down another plate. Holding it up, she said, "See this break on the edge here? It happened when I was 17."

Her voice softened. "One fall day my brothers needed help putting up the last of the fall hay, so they hired a young man to help out. He was slim, with powerful arms and thick blond hair. He had an incredible smile.

"My brothers took a liking to him and invited him to dinner. When my older brother sat the young man next to me, it flustered me so, I nearly fainted."

Suddenly remembering that she was telling the story to her young daughter and a neighbor, Mom blushed and hurried on. "Well, he handed me his plate and asked for a helping. But I was so nervous that when I took the plate, it slipped and knocked against the casserole dish."

"That sounds like a memory I'd try to forget," said Marge.

"Oh, no," countered my mother. "As the young man was leaving, he walked over, took my hand in his and laid a piece of broken china in my palm. He didn't say a word. He just smiled that smile.

"One year later I married him. And to this day, when I see this plate, I fondly recall the moment I met him."

Seeing me staring, Mom gave me a wink. Then, carefully, she put the plate back, behind the others, in a place all its own.

I couldn't forget about that plate with the missing chip. At the first chance, I went up to Mom's room and took out the little wooden jewelry box again. There was the small shard of china.

I examined it carefully, then I ran to the kitchen cupboard, pulled over a chair, climbed up and took down a plate. Just as I had guessed, the chip my mother had so carefully saved belonged to the plate she broke on the day she met my father.

Wiser now, and with more respect, I cautiously returned the chip to its place among the jewels.

The love story that began with that chip is now in its 54th year. Recently one of my sisters asked Mom if someday the antique ruby ring could be hers. My other sister has laid claim to Grandmother's pearl earrings.

As for me, I'd like Mom's most precious keepsake, a memento of an extraordinary life of loving; that little china chip.

The Dance

Thelda Bevens

Dar and I loved to dance. It was probably the first thing we did together, long before we would share our lives.

We grew up in a small Oregon mountain community where dances were held almost every Saturday night, sometimes in the school gym, sometimes at the Grange Hall, sometimes at the home of Nelson Nye. Nelson and his family loved music and dancing so much that they added a special room to their house large enough to accommodate at least three sets of square dancers. Once a month or more, they invited the entire community to a dance. Nelson played the fiddle and his daughter, Hope, played the piano while the rest of us danced.

In those days, the entire family went together—including the grandparents, the farmers and loggers, the school teachers and the store owner. We danced to songs such as "Golden Slippers" and "Red Wing," side-by-side with contemporary ones like "Red Sails in the Sunset" and "It's a Sin to Tell a Lie."

Smaller children always had a place to sleep among the coats, close at hand, when they tired. It was a family affair, one of the few entertainments in a small mountain town climbing slowly out of the Great Depression.

Dar was 17 and I was 12 when we first danced. He was one of the best dancers on the floor and so was I. We always jitterbugged. No slow dancing for us, nothing remotely romantic. Our fathers would stand along the wall and watch. They weren't friends. They didn't talk to each other, not even a casual conversation. Both good dancers themselves, they were proud of their kids. Every once in a while, Dar's dad would smile a little, shake his head and say, to no one in particular, but so my dad could hear, "Boy, my kid can sure dance."

My dad never blinked an eye; acted like he'd never heard. But a while later he would say, to no one in particular, "That girl of mine can sure dance." And being of the old school, they never told us we were that good or had stirred that tiny bit of boastful rivalry along the wall.

Our dancing together stopped for five years while Dar was in the South Pacific in World War II. During those five years, I grew up. When we met again, Dar was 22 and I was almost 18. We began to date—and dance again.

This time it was for ourselves—finding our moves, our turns, our rhythms—adjusting, anticipating, enjoying. We were as good together as we remembered, and this time we added slow dancing to our repertoire.

For us, the metaphor fits. Life is a dance, a movement of rhythms, directions, stumbles, missteps, at times slow and precise, or fast and wild and joyous. We did all the steps.

Two nights before Dar died, the family was with us as they had been for several days—two sons and their wives and four of our eight grandchildren. We all ate dinner together and Dar sat with us. He hadn't been able to eat for several weeks, but he enjoyed it all—told jokes, kidded the boys about their cribbage playing, played with two-year-old Jacob.

Afterward, while the girls were cleaning up the kitchen, I put on a Nat King Cole tape, "Unforgettable." Dar took me in his arms, weak as he was, and we danced.

We held each other and danced and smiled. No tears for us. We were doing what we had loved to do for more than fifty years, and if fate had so ordained, would have gone on doing for fifty more. It was our last dance—forever unforgettable. I wouldn't have missed it for the world.

Don't Forget
What Really Matters

adapted from Paul Harvey

C arl Coleman was driving to work one morning when he bumped fenders with another motorist.

Both cars stopped, and the woman driving the other car got out to survey the damage.

She was distraught. It was her fault, she admitted, and hers was a new car, less than two days from the showroom. She dreaded facing her husband.

Coleman was sympathetic; but he had to pursue the exchange of license and registration data.

She reached into her glove compartment to retrieve the documents in an envelope.

On the first paper to tumble out, written in her husband's distinctive hand, were these words:

"In case of accident, remember, Honey, it's you I love, not the car."

The Last "I Love You"

Debbi Smoot

Carol's husband was killed in an accident last year. Jim, only 52, was driving home from work. The other driver was a teenager with a very high blood-alcohol level. Jim died instantly. The teenager was in the emergency room for less than two hours.

There were other ironic twists: It was Carol's fiftieth birthday, and Jim had two plane tickets to Hawaii in his pocket. He was going to surprise her. Instead, he was killed by a drunk driver.

"How have you survived this?" I finally asked Carol, a year later.

Her eyes welled up with tears. I thought I had said the wrong thing, but she gently took my hand and said, "It's all right, I want to tell you. The day I married Jim, I promised I would never let him leave the house in the morning without telling him I loved him. He made the same promise. It got to be a joke between us, and as babies came along it got to be a hard promise to keep. I remember running down the driveway, saying 'I love you' through teeth clenched when I was mad, or driving to the office to put a note in his car. It was a funny challenge.

"We made a lot of memories trying to say 'I love you' before noon every day of our married life.

"The morning Jim died, he left a birthday card in the kitchen and slipped out to the car. I heard the engine starting. *Oh, no, you don't buster*, I thought. I raced out and banged on the car window until he rolled it down. 'Here on my fiftieth birthday, Mr. James E. Garret, I, Carol Garret, want to go on record as saying I love you!'

"That's how I've survived. Knowing that the last words I said to Jim were, 'I LOVE YOU!'"

LOVE

*Love never asks how much must I do,
but how much can I do.*

Frederick A. Agar

Family

A MOMENT IN TIME

He climbed onto the seat and positioned his feet on the pedals, his hands on the handle bars.

"Don't let go," he ordered.

"I'll be right next to you," I assured him. "I won't let you fall...."

I thought of the days ahead—of times when I would show my son balance, when I would run alongside him, when I would be there to hold him, and when I would have to let go again and again.

Matthew Norquist

When Grown Kids Come to Visit

Erma Bombeck

In earlier days, I was a mother who made her kids pick up their rooms, make their own snacks and put their laundry in the utility room. Now when they come home, I put the rules aside. I am like a concierge looking for a big tip. I follow them around asking, "Are you hungry? Can I get you something? Do you have laundry?"

I eat when they want to eat, cook their favorite foods just before they tell me they are going out with friends and watch helplessly as they eat their way through a pound of baked ham at three in the afternoon.

On their visit, my life changes. I have no car. My washer is set at extra-large load and has two socks and a T-shirt in it. The phone rings constantly and is never for me.

At the end of their visits, we set aside a day, pack a lunch and head for the airport. It isn't until I return home that I sense how orderly my life has become. I enjoy the quiet. The TV tuner is rescued from the clothes hamper and is returned to its place on the coffee table. The empty milk and juice cartons are removed from the refrigerator. The wet towels are put in the washer. The bathroom is returned to health standards.

It is my world again. So why am I crying?

Running Away

Christopher de Vinck

I had finally had it. The children were loud, cranky, impossible. I was tired and fed up. My wife was tired and fed up. I decided that I was going to run away from it all and have a day just for me. I wanted to spoil myself. I wanted to have a day in which I did just what I wanted to do. I was going to live it up and be as greedy as I pleased. I wasn't going to tend to anyone except myself.

I zoomed out of the house with fifty dollars. *There! I did it!* I said to myself as I drove to the highway and headed north.

Well, I drove to a mall and had a wild time in a bookstore and bought the collected poems of Walt Whitman. After that I drove and drove to a McDonald's and ordered *two* hamburgers, my *own* large fries, and my *own* large soda. I ate everything *without* being interrupted, without giving my pickle to *anyone*, without wiping someone's mouth, nose, lap. Then I bought the *biggest* chocolate ice cream I could find.

I was free. I was out of town, so I drove to a movie theater and watched a movie without buying popcorn, without someone sitting on my lap, without escorting someone to the bathroom. I was a free man. I was living it up. And I was miserable.

By the time I had returned home, everyone was asleep. As I slipped into bed, my wife whispered, "We missed you."

"Me, too," I answered. I never ran away from home again.

Why My Wife Bought Handcuffs

Philip Gulley

When I was twenty-three years old, I made the best decision of my life. I asked a beautiful, witty woman to be my wife, and she accepted, against the advice of her friends, her family, and a goodly portion of the Western world. On our wedding day, the bridesmaids wore black.

For eight years, I was the model of responsibility. I worked hard. I dried the dishes. I lowered the toilet seat. Then my wife became pregnant. I attended birthing classes and learned to commiserate. When we brought Spencer home, I rose with her to feed him. And when he regurgitated on me, I bore it with good humor.

Three months after his birth, Joan returned to part-time work. On the morning of her departure, she cautioned me to keep a close eye on our son. My feelings were hurt, and I said as much.

"Please, honey, haven't I proven myself reliable?" Thus, I can only think it was the pain of mistrust which caused me to forget my son when I went to the grocery store that afternoon.

I was on my way there and turned around to see him. He was missing! I raced home and found him in his crib, glowering, and I knew what he was going to say when he learned to talk. So I confessed to Joan myself, over a candlelight dinner and new silver bracelet.

Being a Christian woman, Joan forgave me and offered me another chance. And the very next morning, after she handcuffed me to Spencer, she said, "Honey, I trust you."

Reflection on this experience has taught me two things: first, having children causes irreparable damage to those areas of the brain having to do with memory; and second, uh, what's the second point? Oh, yeah, the second point is this: we all feel forgotten sometimes.

Actually, I'd learned that second lesson at an early age. My family drove off and forgot me once, too. We were on vacation—five kids, Mom, and Dad—and stopped to eat at a Stuckey's. I was in the bathroom when they climbed back in the car and headed out. They went twenty miles before discovering they were short a kid. Took a quick vote and decided to come back for me. It was almost a tie, but at the last minute Mom changed her mind.

So sometimes each of us feels forgotten. Saddest line in the Bible is when Christ asks God why he forsook him. If Christ felt left behind, how then can we avoid feeling forgotten and forsaken?

Some Bible scholars say that isn't what Jesus meant when he cried from the cross. They say he was quoting the first line of Psalm 22, because to quote the first line was to affirm that psalm's victorious conclusion. I have a great deal of respect for Bible scholars, but they're full of baloney on this one. I think Jesus felt forgotten.

However, the empty tomb tells us he was remembered. And so are we all, which is what I'm going to tell my son, just as soon as I remember where I left him.

Too Busy

Ron Mehl

I'll never forget the day I looked out of our living room and saw Mark, our youngest, walking home from school in the driving rain. Mark was in third grade, and he was allowed to ride his bike to his grade school, located right within our subdivision. I happened to be home from the church early that day, and I was sitting in an easy chair by the window. I looked outside at the pouring rain and saw my boy in the distance, trudging his way through the downpour. His clothing was absolutely drenched and his hair was plastered against his head. I opened the door for him, and he looked up at me with a little smile, his face red from the cold.

"Hi, Dad!" he said. "You're home early."

"Hi, Son," I replied. "You're soaked to the skin."

"Yeah, I know."

"Umm, Mark, you know, if you'd ride your bike you'd get home faster. You wouldn't get so wet."

He looked at me rather sheepishly as rivulets of rain streamed from his hair down across his face. "I know, Dad."

I was puzzled. "Well, Son, if you *know*, why in the world didn't you do it?"

Then he hung his head, just a bit, and it hit me. Boy, did I feel like crawling under a table and hiding for a while. He had told me several times before that his bike had a flat tire. He had asked me, "Dad, could you please fix it for me?"

"Sure, Son," I'd promised him. "Don't worry. I'll get after it right away." But I never did. I'd forgotten all about it.

As he stood there in the entryway, dripping and shivering, he could have said, "I couldn't ride my bike today because someone promised me he'd fix it and never did." He would have had every right to say that. But he didn't. What he did say remains printed indelibly on this dad's heart.

"Aw, Dad, I know how busy you are and everything, and—I just didn't want to bother you with it again."

I thought, *Son, your dad isn't too busy; he's just too selfish.*

For me, a bike tire was no big deal—just one more thing on a long "to do" list. But for Mark, it meant more than transportation. It meant more than a long walk home in the rain. It meant trusting his father to meet his every need.

When the Moon Doesn't Shine

Ruth Senter

Usually the moon shines bright on clear May nights in eastern Pennsylvania. But tonight the moon is missing. All is dark. I notice brown circles under the lamp in the hall when Mother welcomes our 2:00 a.m. arrival from Illinois. I also notice brown circles under her eyes. Spots I'd never noticed before. Tired skin under gentle folds.

But here she stands, my mother of forty years. I sense an accumulation of nights waiting up for home-coming children, as though the years have cast shadows from the lamp onto her face. I see the years in the black and blue veins that have just this week felt the heart specialist's probe. I hear the years—like the ocean ringing in a seashell—in the doctor's diagnosis. "Red flag...enlarged heart...slow the pace...." I stare into uncertainty. Mother has been a steady pulse through the years. Tomorrow has been an assumed promise—a grand procession of family weddings, births, graduations, music recitals, ordinations, Christmas, Easter, Thanksgiving. Time has been an event, not a sequence.

As I look at Mother, I sense that someone has wound the clock. Time now has a cadence. Years have become increments. History has a beginning and an end. I shiver in the early morning chill. But then Mother's arms wrap me in warmth, and I am home. A forty-year-old child reassured by her mother's touch. There is no time in touch. Welcoming arms know not the years.

I hear the tea kettle whistling. Freshly baked chocolate chip cookies wait on the old ironstone plate that once served cookies from Grandma Hollinger's kitchen. Mother's chocolate chip cookies and Grandma Hollinger's ironstone plate pull me back into timelessness. We sip peppermint tea and laugh over a silly story Dad tells. Our laughter drowns out the clock. There is no time in laughter. Mother laughs the hardest of all. Dark circles. Tired circles of joy. Her children are home.

For a moment I forget bruised veins and ticking clocks. I am held together by things that do not change—a mother's early morning welcome, freshly baked chocolate chip cookies, an ironstone plate, peppermint tea, a mantel clock, and laughter. I am held together by a God who does not change. I know the God of time who is yet above time. I see tonight in my mother's face the strange paradox of time and timelessness. A rare glimpse of the divine.

Father's Day: A Tribute

Max Lucado

Today is Father's Day. A day of cologne. A day of hugs, new neckties, long-distance phone calls, and Hallmark cards.

Today is my first Father's Day without a father. For thirty-one years I had one. I had one of the best. But now he's gone. He's buried under an oak tree in a west Texas cemetery. Even though he's gone, his presence is very near—especially today.

It seems strange that he isn't here. I guess that's because he was never gone. He was always close by. Always available. Always present. His words were nothing novel. His achievements, though admirable, were nothing extraordinary.

But his presence was.

Like a warm fireplace in a large house, he was a source of comfort. Like a sturdy porch swing or a big-branched elm in the backyard, he could always be found...and leaned upon.

During the turbulent years of my adolescence, Dad was one part of my life that was predictable. Girl friends came and girl friends went, but Dad was there. Football season turned into baseball season and turned into football season again and Dad was always there. Summer vacation, Homecoming dates, algebra, first car, driveway basketball—they all had one thing in common: his presence.

And because he was there life went smoothly. The car always ran, the bills got paid, and the lawn stayed mowed. Because he was there the laughter was fresh and the future was secure. Because he was there my growing up was what God intended growing up to be; a storybook scamper through the magic and mystery of the world.

Because he was there we kids never worried about things

like income tax, savings accounts, monthly bills, or mortgages. Those were the things on Daddy's desk.

We have lots of family pictures without him. Not because he wasn't there, but because he was always behind the camera.

He made the decisions, broke up the fights, chuckled at Archie Bunker, read the paper every evening, and fixed breakfast on Sundays. He didn't do anything unusual. He only did what dads are supposed to do—be there.

He taught me how to shave and how to pray. He helped me memorize verses for Sunday school and taught me that wrong should be punished and that rightness has its own reward. He modeled the importance of getting up early and staying out of debt. His life expressed the elusive balance between ambition and self-acceptance.

He comes to mind often. When I smell "Old Spice" aftershave, I think of him. When I see a bass boat I see his face. And occasionally, not too often, but occasionally when I hear a good joke, (the kind Red Skelton would tell), I hear him chuckle. He had a copyright chuckle that always came with a wide grin and arched eyebrows.

Daddy never said a word to me about sex or told me his life story. But I knew that if I ever wanted to know, he would tell me. All I had to do was ask. And I knew if I ever needed him, he'd be there.

Like a warm fireplace.

Maybe that's why this Father's Day is a bit chilly. The fire has gone out. The winds of age swallowed the late splendid flame, leaving only golden embers. But there is a strange thing about those embers, stir them a bit and a flame will dance. It will dance only briefly, but it will dance. And it will knock just enough chill out of the air to remind me that he is still...in a special way, very present.

Releasing the Arrow

Stu Weber

As I write these words, I'm looking at three arrows on my desk. They differ from one another. Any archer could see that at a glance. Yet in other ways they are remarkably similar.

I'm turning one in my hand, now. Feeling the heft and balance of its shaft. Looking down its length to the round edges of its blunt head. It's a target arrow, and a good one. I wouldn't waste my time with anything less. It has plastic vanes instead of feathers—the kind of arrow you'd want for shooting in rainy western Oregon. This second one now…yes, it has a good feel to it, too. A hunting arrow. Smooth shaft. Well balanced. A slightly heavier head, and crafted to a literal razor's edge. It's a "broadhead." Plastic-vaned and intended for wet country hunting. The third one is the kind I carry east of the mountains, over on the dry side. It's basically a twin of the second arrow, but it sports neat black and gray feathers instead of plastic.

They're different, these arrows of mine. Each intended for a different impact. Each designed for a different sort of target. They're also very similar; each has been fashioned and crafted, molded and balanced. They're all intended for flight. They're all intended for a target. They're all intended for maximum impact on that target.

They're good arrows. But then again, they're not much better than the archer who notches them on the bow. They're not much better than the fullness of his draw. They're not much better than the smoothness of his release. No matter how finely crafted those arrows might be, you couldn't pull a guy off the street and expect him to let loose with a seventy-pound bow and nail a target with one of them. Accuracy demands a trained, full draw and a disciplined release.

As I write these words, I'm looking at a picture on my desk.

It's a picture of my three sons—Kent, Blake, and Ryan. They're different, these sons of mine. Unbelievably different. But they're also similar.

Each was crafted by the Lord God in the secret place of his mother's womb. And each was fashioned, balanced, and readied for flight within the four walls of our home.

My three arrows were all designed to leap from the bow and split the air. I enjoy bow hunting, and I intend to use these arrows—whether on a cedar bale target or on a bull elk stamping on some back-country ridge on a frosty morning. These arrows aren't for show. They were never intended to stay in the quiver. The quiver is just a vehicle that carries them until they are ready for release. You might say those arrows were made to be released. They were made to play. They were made to pierce a target.

So it is with my three sons. They were never intended to stay bunched in the four walls of their childhood home. Yes, the home is a vehicle to fashion and straighten and true and balance those boys. But when the moment comes...young men—and young women—were made to experience flight.

Laughter in the Walls

Bob Benson

I pass a lot of houses
on my way home.
Some pretty,
some expensive,
some inviting.

But my heart always skips a beat
when I turn down the road
and see my house
nestled against the hill.

I guess I'm especially proud
of the house
and the way it looks
because I drew the plans myself.
It started out large enough for us—
I even had a study,
two teenage boys
now reside in there.
And it had a guest room,
my girl and nine dolls
are permanent guests.
It had a small room
Peg had hoped
would be her sewing room,
the two boys swinging
on the Dutch door
have claimed this room as their own.

So it really doesn't look right now
as if I'm much of an architect.
But it will get larger again.

One by one they will go away—
to work, to college,
to service,
to their own houses.
And then there will be room—
a guest room, a study,
and a sewing room—
just for the two of us.

But it won't be empty.
Every corner, every room,
every nick in the coffee table
will be crowded
with memories.
Memories of picnics,
parties, Christmases,
bedside vigils, summers,
fires, winters, going barefoot,
leaving for vacation, cats,
conversations, black eyes,
graduations, first dates,
ball games, arguments,
washing dishes, bicycles,
dogs, boat rides,
getting home from vacation,
meals, rabbits,
and a thousand other things
that fill the lives
of those who would raise five.

And Peg and I
will sit quietly by the fire
and listen to the
laughter in the walls.

WALK PLAINER

Walk a little plainer, Daddy! I know that once you walked this way many years ago, and what you did along the way I'd really like to know; for sometimes when I am tempted, I don't know what to do. So walk a little plainer, Daddy, for I must follow you.

Author Unknown

Dad's Helper

Ron Mehl

A little boy was helping his father move some books out of an attic into more spacious quarters downstairs. It was important to this little boy that he was helping his dad, even though he was probably getting in the way and slowing things down more than he was actually assisting. But that boy had a wise and patient father who knew it was more important to work at a task with his young son than it was to move a pile of books efficiently.

Among this man's books, however, were some rather large study books, and it was a chore for the boy to get them down the stairs. As a matter of fact, on one particular load, the boy dropped his pile of books several times. Finally, he sat down on the stairs and wept in frustration. He wasn't doing any good at all. He wasn't strong enough to carry the big books down a narrow stairway. It hurt him to think he couldn't do this for his daddy.

Without a word, the father picked up the dropped load of books, put them into the boy's arms, and scooped up both the boy and the books into his arms and carried them down the stairs. And so they continued for load after load, both enjoying each other's company very much. The boy carrying the books, the dad carrying the boy.

Legacy of an Adopted Child

Author Unknown

Once there were two women who never knew each other.
One you do not remember, the other you call Mother.
Two different lives shaped to make your one.
One became your guiding star, the other became your sun.
The first one gave you life, and the second taught you to
    live it.
The first gave you a need for love, and the second was there
    to give it.
One gave you a nationality, the other gave you a name.
One gave you the seed of talent, the other gave you aim.
One gave you emotions, the other calmed your fears.
One saw your first sweet smile, the other dried your tears.
One sought for you a home that she could not provide,
The other prayed for a child and her hope was not denied.
And now you ask me through your tears
The age-old question through the years,
Heredity or environment—
Which are you the product of?
Neither, my darling—neither;
Just two different kinds of love.

The Gift

George Parler

It was our turn to open our presents this particular Christmas morning. The living room was already covered with torn wrapping paper from the onslaught of the children's eagerness to unveil the hidden treasures that had tormented them for nearly a month. Now we adults sat around the room with our presents at our feet, slowly removing the paper while at the same time holding back the child within ourselves and maintaining our dignity in front of each other.

My wife, Brenda, and her family have a tradition of getting each other gag gifts. This always makes me a bit uneasy at Christmas or my birthday, never knowing what form of embarrassment lies waiting for me under the thin confines of the wrapping paper.

One of my daughters, Christy, who at the time was six years old, was standing directly in front of me. The excitement of the moment just beamed across her face. It was everything she could do to keep herself from helping me rip the paper from each present. Finally, I came to the last gift. And with my natural Sherlock Holmes ability, I deduced that this had to be the gag gift. Because with them it was never a question of "if," it was a question of when you came to it. So, with everyone looking on, I decided to go ahead and get it over with—just let them have their laugh—and I ripped off the paper. And there it was...a toy airplane about two inches long. Our holiday guests started giggling to themselves as I looked up to my wife with a smirk on my face and blurted out, "A toy airplane, give me a break!"

Brenda gave me the look—that look that always tells me I have just put my foot in my mouth and am in the process of thoroughly chewing it. I had failed to look at the name tag before I opened the present to see who it was from. As I picked up the paper from the floor and read the name tag, my heart sank. On the tag were scribbled block letters that read, "To Dad, Love Christy." I have never felt as low at any time in my life as I did at that moment. One of the most agonizing experiences of my life was having to look down into her little face to find the joy that had once been there replaced with a look of total embarrassment and humiliation. The fear in her eyes spoke her thoughts of hoping no one would find out that the gift her father found so repulsive had come from her.

This loving child had taken her spending money that she could have spent on herself, but she had chosen instead to buy her daddy a Christmas present. And it wasn't just *any* present. She knew from watching me play computer video flight-simulator games that I was fascinated with airplanes.

I quickly knelt down and grabbed her up in my arms and held her as tight as I possibly could, willing to give anything to be able to take back those words. I made a feeble attempt to explain that I thought it had come from Mom, but since I found out it came from her, that made it different. It was obvious that nothing I could say was going to change the hurt in her little heart. I had to find a way to prove I meant what I said.

And I did. I took that toy airplane in my hand and began making airplane noises. I taxied onto the runway, which was the counter, and throttled to full thrust and was soon airborne. My mission goal was to remove the hurt from my baby's face—that I had caused—and to continue until her smile returned. I played all day with that airplane. I put so much excitement into that airplane that the other children left their new Christmas toys and wanted a turn playing with my little two-inch airplane. And just like a little selfish kid I said, "No, this is mine!" It wasn't very long until Christy's face was beaming with a smile again. But I didn't stop there. That little plane became a treasure of great wealth to me, and still is, for I still have that little two-inch plane.

I keep that plane mainly because it came from my little girl's heart with love. But it's also a reminder to me of the power of words.

FITTING DESCRIPTION

There are many ways to measure success;
not the least of which is the way your child describes you
when talking to a friend.

Author Unknown

Papa's Sermon

Author Unknown

Busy in his study, a minister was preparing his sermon for the coming Sunday. He reached to the shelf at his side for a book, and then remembered that he had left it downstairs. His little daughter was playing in the bedroom, and he called her. She came, running, eager and delighted at the thought that Papa needed her. He explained carefully where she could find the book, and she went gladly, returning in a moment with a book which he saw at a glance was the wrong one. But he hardly looked at the book as he took it and laid it on the table. He looked only at the eager face of his daughter, wreathed in smiles. Gathering her close to his heart, he kissed her and said, "Thank you, darling." And when she had gone back happy and contented to her play he went quietly for the book he needed. I think I should like to listen to the sermons that man would preach.

Alone Time for Mom

Crystal Kirgiss

All I needed this morning was a half-hour alone, thirty minutes of peace and quiet to help preserve my sanity. No mom-do-this, mom-I-need-that, mom-he-hit-me, mom-I-spilled-juice-on-the-couch.

Just me, a hot Calgon bath, and nothingness.

I shouldn't dream so big.

After getting the two oldest off to school, I settled the youngest in front of Barney and said, "Honey, listen closely. Your mommy is going to crack. She's losing her marbles. She's teetering on the edge of permanent personality damage. This is because she has children. Are you following me so far?"

He nodded absently while singing, "Barney is a dinosaur in our imagination...."

"Good. Now, if you want to be a good little boy, you'll sit right here and watch Barney while Mommy takes a nice, hot, quiet, peaceful, take-me-away bath. I don't want you to bother me. I want you to leave me alone. For 30 minutes, I don't want to see you or hear you. Got it?"

Nod.

"Good morning, boys and girls..." I heard the purple wonder say.

I headed to the bathroom with my fingers crossed.

I watched the water fill the tub. I watched the mirror and window steam up. I watched the water turn blue from my bath beads. I got in.

I heard a knock on the door.

"Mom? Mom? Are you in there, Mom?!"

I learned long ago that ignoring my children does not make them go away.

"Yes, I'm in here. What do you want?"

There was a long pause while the child tried to decide what he wanted.

"Um…can I have a snack?"

"You just had breakfast! Can't you wait a few minutes?"

"No, I'm dying! I need a snack right now!"

"Fine. You can have a box of raisins."

I heard him pad off to the kitchen, listened as he pushed chairs and stools around trying to reach the raisin shelf, felt the floor vibrate when he jumped off the counter, and heard him run back to the TV room.

"Hi, Susie! Can you tell me what color the grass is…?"

Knock, knock, knock.

"Mom? Mom? Are you in there, Mom?!"

Sigh. "Yes, I'm still in here. What do you need now?"

Pause. "Um…I need to take a bath, too."

Right.

"Honey, can't you wait until I'm done?"

The door opened just a crack.

"No, I really need to take one now. I'm dirty."

"You're always dirty! Since when do you care?"

The door opened all the way.

"I really need to take a bath, Mom."

"No, you don't. Go away."

He stood in the middle of the bathroom and started taking off his pajamas.

"I'll just get in with you and take a bath, too."

"No! You will not get in with me and take a bath! I want to take my own bath! I want you to go away and leave me alone!" I began to sound like the three-year-old with whom I was arguing.

He climbed onto the edge of the tub, balancing carefully, and said, "I'll just get in *with* you, okay, Mom?"

I started to shriek, "No! That is not okay! I want my own bath, all by myself! I don't want to share! I want to be alone!"

He thought for a moment and said, "Okay. I'll just sit here and you can read me a book. I won't get in, Mom, until you're done." He flashed me a knock-down charming smile.

So I spent my morning-alone-time reading *One Fish, Two Fish* to a naked three-year-old who sat on the edge of the tub with his chin resting on his knees, arms wrapped around his bent legs, slight smile on his face.

Why fight it? It won't be long before I have all the alone-time I want. And then I'll probably feel bad about not having any more together-time.

Words for Your Family

Gary Smalley and John Trent

I'm proud of you.
Way to go!
Bingo—you did it.
Magnificent.
I knew you could do it.
What a good helper.
You're very special to me.
I trust you.
What a treasure.
Hurray for you!
Beautiful work.
You're a real trooper.
Well done.
That's so creative.
You make my day.
You're a joy.
Give me a big hug.
You're such a good listener.
You figured it out.
I love you.
You're so responsible.
You remembered.
You're the best.
You sure tried hard.
I've got to hand it to you.
I couldn't be prouder of you.
You light up my day.

My buttons are popping off.
I'm praying for you.
You're wonderful.
I'm behind you.

FAIR EXCHANGE

*Let the wife make the husband glad to come home, and let him
make her sorry to see him leave.*

Martin Luther

Gift of Love

James Dobson

Some time ago, a friend of mine punished his three-year-old daughter for wasting a roll of gold wrapping paper. Money was tight, and he became infuriated when the child tried to decorate a box to put under the Christmas tree. Nevertheless, the little girl brought the gift to her father the next morning and said, "This is for you, Daddy." He was embarrassed by his earlier over-reaction, but his anger flared again when he found that the box was empty.

He yelled at her, "Don't you know that when you give someone a present, there's supposed to be something inside of it?"

The little girl looked up at him with tears in her eyes and said, "Oh, Daddy, it's not empty. I blew kisses in the box. I filled it with my love. All for you, Daddy."

The father was crushed. He put his arms around his little girl, and he begged her for forgiveness. My friend told me that he kept that gold box by his bed for years. Whenever he was discouraged, he would take out an imaginary kiss and remember the love of the child who had put it there.

In a very real sense, each of us as parents has been given a gold container filled with unconditional love and kisses from our children. There is no more precious possession anyone could hold.

A Mother's Way

Temple Bailey

The young mother set her foot on the path of life. "Is the way long?"

"Yes," her Guide said, "and the way is hard. You will be old before you reach the end of it. But—" He stopped to smile warmly. "The end will be better than the beginning."

The young mother was so happy, though, that she could not believe anything could be better than these early years. She played with her children, and gathered flowers for them along the way, and bathed with them in the clear streams. The sun shone on them and life was good, and the young mother cried, "Nothing will ever be lovelier than this."

Then night came, and storm, and the path was dark. The children shook with fear and cold, and the mother drew them close, covering them with her mantle. Her children said, "Oh, Mother, we are not afraid when you are near." The mother said, "This is better than the brightness of day, for I have taught my children courage."

Then the morning came, and there was a hill ahead. The children climbed and grew weary. The mother was weary, too, but she kept encouraging her children, "A little patience and we are there." So the children continued to climb. When they reached the top, they said, "We could not have done it without you, Mother." And the mother, when she lay down that night, looked past the stars and said, "This is a better day than the last. My children have learned fortitude in the face of difficulty. Yesterday I taught them courage, today I have taught them strength."

With the next day came strange clouds that darkened the earth—clouds of war and hate and evil. The children groped and stumbled. The mother said, "Look up. Lift your eyes past the blackness to the Light." The children looked up and saw an Everlasting Glory above the strange clouds. It guided them and brought them through the darkness and evil. That night the mother said, "This is the best day of all, for I have helped my children learn to see God."

The days went on, and the weeks and the months and the years. The mother grew old, until she was very little and bent. But her children were tall and strong, and they walked with courage. When the way was hard, they helped their mother; when the way was rough, they lifted her, for she was as light as a feather. At last they came to a hill, and beyond the hill they could see a shining road and golden gate flung wide.

The mother said, "I have reached the end of my journey. Now I know that the end really is better than the beginning, for my children can walk alone, and they will teach their children after them."

The children said, "You will always walk with us, Mother, even when you have gone through the gates."

They stood and watched her as she went on alone, and the gates closed after her. They said, "We can't see her, but she is with us still. A mother like ours is more than a memory."

Tender Intuition

Robin Jones Gunn

I hold you in my arms, young prince. You sleep in sweet, heavenly peace. Yet, I wonder if you'd be so calm if you knew the truth: I am your mother. And I don't have the slightest idea what I'm doing. You are my first baby ever. My only son. I was just getting used to being pregnant, and now here you are! And you are so very, very real.

I've been preparing for your arrival for months. I've read the books. Well, some of them. A few pages. I've listened to my friends who give me endless advice. They're all experienced, you know, because they have their own babies. But you're different. You're my baby. And they don't know a thing about you.

I do. I know all about the way you kick and wiggle. I've already memorized the way you smell, like a fresh-from-the-earth daffodil. I know about the way your lower lip quivers when you're about to cry. I know that your wispy hair is the most luxuriously soft thing that has ever touched my cheek.

Yet I admit, there's much I don't know. In the hospital I had to be instructed on how to nurse you. Yesterday my mother showed me how to bathe you in the sink. I don't have a clue how to clear up diaper rash. I get queasy at the sight of blood. I don't sew. I'm not good at salt dough maps. My math skills are atrocious. And you might as well know right up—that wiggly teeth give me the heebie-jeebies.

However, I am very good at baking cookies. I know how to make indoor tents on rainy days. And I have my father's wonderful sense of humor so I know how to laugh and how to make you laugh.

I'll sing you sweet songs in the night. I'll pray for you every day. I'll let you keep any animal you catch, as long as you can feed it. I'll call all your imaginary friends by their first names. I'll put love notes in your lunch box, and I'll swim in the ocean with you, even when I'm old.

Perhaps my best qualification to be your mother is that I share this privilege with the most incredible man in the world—your father.

Such secrets of motherhood can't be learned over coffee with friends. They can't be taught by a book, or even by trial and error. To me, these tender intuitions are what matter most. Eternal insights only a mother can know—when her baby is in her arms as you are now in mine. This is where the Lord will teach me how to mother you by heart.

Slippery Risks

Heather Harpham Kopp

Several days ago my mother came for a visit. Before she left, you might say she was all wet. She would say I was.

Tom and I took her to our local swimming pool with a long, winding waterslide. We urged her to try it, telling her what great, safe fun it was.

She hesitated, reminding me that she's never even jumped off a diving board.

I wasn't shocked. My mother's always been shy, and never much of a risk-taker. Her idea of a risk is to drive past a garage sale without stopping.

But daughters have powerful manipulative skills with their mothers, and I am no exception.

Before she could change her mind, Tom hurried her to the top of the slide. When her face turned white just before takeoff, Tom tried to reassure her. He said she could go as slow as she wanted. And he reminded her that no one had ever flown out of a waterslide—or at least not this one in particular.

All we can figure is that she must have doubted this. She must have decided the safest thing was to lie flat, toes pointed, and try to avoid ejection.

I watched from the bottom. But my mother thundered down that slide so fast I almost didn't see her. You have to understand that my mom is not a small woman. She is 5'7", and as she puts it, "has eaten her share of the leftovers."

Yet who could miss her wide-open mouth, her shocked expression? When she shot out the end, her glasses, which she'd carefully tucked inside her bosom, came flying out. In fact, the slide had to be shut down so the lifeguards could help my mortified and now half-blind mother find her spectacles.

I felt bad. But I had learned at an early age that life isn't worth living without taking a few risks. And sometimes people need a little prodding. If you're lucky, they'll thank you. If you're not, make sure they can't find you in the crowded pool.

I got my first lesson on risking when I was five. A nine-year-old neighbor girl wanted me to drop another boy's toy gun into the mailbox that sat kitty-corner from our house. I had no qualms about doing this girl's dirty-work, but I told her I wasn't allowed to cross the street.

"Why don't I just carry you, then?" she said with confidence. "That way, you won't *really* be crossing the street."

Well, that sounded good to me.

So I got the kid's toy gun and dropped it in the mailbox. But on the way back, my accomplice accidentally dropped me upside down on the pavement—my third set of stitches that summer.

That's the problem with risks. Not all risks should be taken, and not all prodding should be listened to. This is what my mom said back then, and also when she found me at the pool, hiding in the kiddie section.

Usually the risks we *need* to take aren't the kind that chance a stitch or two to our head, anyway. They're the kind that risk a blow to our pride. Like a ride down a slide. Or a romance. Or admitting an unattractive truth about ourselves. In fact, some things are impossible to gain without risks: experience, love, honesty, adventure.

My mother must be learning the same thing. It's the only explanation I can fathom. Would you believe that after she recovered from her traumatic trip down the slide, and after she forgave me, she announced she wanted to try it again?

"You're kidding!" I said, incredulous.

"Only this time," she said, "I'll sit up, hold onto the sides, and go down slowly."

Of course, my mom fell flat onto her back as soon as she shoved off. And for all of her frantic gesturing and flailing, she couldn't manage to sit back up again.

I stood at the bottom of the slide waiting for my risk-taking mother. And for the first time in my life, I asked God to make me more like her.

Mother's arms are made for tenderness,
and sweet sleep blesses the child
who lies therein.

Victor Hugo

Family Vacations and Other Threats to Marriage

Philip Gulley

When our son, Spencer, was six weeks old, I said to my wife, "It's time for a vacation."

"Not a good idea," she cautioned. But she went along because she believes in me learning from my mistakes.

We went to a lodge four hours away. Spencer slept the whole way there. I was gloating. Checked in. Went to our room. I was gloating some more. Having kids is a breeze. Moms are such alarmists.

Then Spencer woke up.

In the book of Revelation, John writes about the seven plagues of divine wrath, ranging from bodily sores to earthquakes. John missed a plague—crying kids.

Spencer stopped crying long enough for us to eat dinner. Grandmother-types looked at us and smiled. Before I had a child, I thought they smiled because they liked children. I understand now that they smile because their children are grown.

We went back to our room and went to bed. Spencer cried all night. The next morning at breakfast we tried to slip out of the restaurant without him, but the manager blocked our escape.

What happened on the way home can only be attributed to sleep deprivation. In an effort to salvage our first family vacation, I drove home on a designated scenic route. The state calls them "scenic routes" because it can't squeeze "twisty-road-that-adds-three-hours-to-your-trip-and-makes-your-kid-carsick route" on one sign.

The next year at vacation time, having forgotten our previous vacation, we drove to a lodge eight hours away. Spencer didn't cry once. He slept soundlessly every night. He rode in his car-seat without complaint. We didn't hear a peep from him, but then earplugs have that effect.

That family vacations don't turn out like we'd hoped can only be blamed on television and its inaccurate portrayal of family life. I remember a *Brady Bunch* episode when the Bradys traveled for an entire week without once having to stop to use the bathroom. Florence Henderson sang across three states without anyone pushing her out the car door. When I was growing up, we wouldn't be out of the driveway before my brother Glenn had slugged me for breathing on him.

We do ourselves a disfavor when we expect family life to be *The Brady Bunch* revisited. Truth is, most of our families lurch from one mess to another. And that's not an altogether bad thing. Otherwise, how would we cultivate the fine art of forgiveness?

My wife even forgave me after our first vacation. She said at the time, "You can't help it. You come from a long line of men who don't listen to their wives."

We're saving up for our next vacation. We're thinking about the mountains.

"There're all kinds of places to lose a kid there," I told my wife. But she knows I'm just kidding.

Actually, I thank God every day for my children. Every day, just some days more than others.

When God Created Fathers

Erma Bombeck

When the good Lord was creating fathers, He started with a tall frame.

A female angel nearby said, "What kind of father is that? If you're going to make children so close to the ground, why have you put fathers up so high? He won't be able to shoot marbles without kneeling, tuck a child in bed without bending or even kiss a child without a lot of stooping."

And God smiled and said, "Yes, but if I make him child-size, who would children have to look up to?"

And when God made a father's hands, they were large and sinewy.

The angel shook her head sadly and said, "Large hands are clumsy. They can't manage diaper pins, small buttons, rubber bands on ponytails or even remove splinters caused by baseball bats."

And God smiled and said, "I know, but they're large enough to hold everything a small boy empties from his pockets at the end of a day, yet small enough to cup a child's face."

And then God molded long, slim legs and broad shoulders.

The angel nearly had a heart attack. "Boy, this is the end of the week, all right," she clucked. "Do you realize you just made a father without a lap? How is he going to pull a child close to him without the kid falling between his legs?"

And God smiled and said, "A mother needs a lap. A father needs strong shoulders to pull a sled, balance a boy on a bicycle or hold a sleepy head on the way home from the circus."

God was in the middle of creating two of the largest feet anyone had ever seen when the angel could contain herself no longer. "That's not fair. Do you honestly think those large boats are going to dig out of bed early in the morning when the baby cries? Or walk through a small birthday party without crushing at least three of the guests?"

And God smiled and said, "They'll work. You'll see. They'll support a small child who wants to ride a horse to Banbury Cross or scare off mice at the summer cabin or display shoes that will be a challenge to fill."

God worked throughout the night, giving the father few words but a firm, authoritative voice and eyes that saw everything but remained calm and tolerant.

Finally, almost as an afterthought, He added tears. Then He turned to the angel and said, "Now, are you satisfied that he can love as much as a mother?"

The angel shutteth up.

Life

NO BOX

There is no box
made by God
nor us
but that the sides can be flattened out
and the top blown off
to make a dance floor
on which to celebrate life.

Kenneth Caraway

Lookin' Good

Patsy Clairmont

I remember the day well. It was one of those times when everything goes right. I took a shower and fixed my hair. It went just the way I wanted it to, as it seldom does. I pulled on my new pink sweater, giving me added color, since I need all the help I can get. I pulled on my gray slacks and my taupe heels.

I checked the mirror and thought, *Lookin' good!*

Since it was a cool Michigan day, I slipped on my gray trench coat with pink on the lapels. I was color-coded from head to toe.

When I arrived in downtown Brighton, where I intended to take care of some errands, I was surprised to find heavy traffic. Brighton is a small town, but it has a large health food store. Usually, I can park right in front and run in.

But today business was so brisk I had to park two blocks away. When your attitude is right, and it's a great day, however, inconveniences and interruptions are no big deal.

I thought, *I'll just bounce down the street in time to the sunshine.*

I got out of the car, bounced down the street, crossed the road and entered the store.

As I headed toward the back of the store, I caught my reflection in the glass doors of the refrigeration system. It reaffirmed I was lookin' good. While enjoying my mirrored self, I noticed something was following me. I turned and realized it was my panty hose!

I remembered the night before when I had done a little Wonder Woman act and taken panty hose and slacks off in one fell swoop. This morning I put on new pantyhose and must have pushed the old panty hose through when I pulled on my slacks.

I believe they made their emergence as I bounced down the street in time to the sunshine. I remembered the truck driver who stopped his truck to let me cross. As I looked up, he was laughing, and I thought, *Oh, look! The whole world is happy today!*

So I waved. Little did I realize how much I was waving.

I assumed I had reached some amount of maturity by this time in my life, but I can honestly say that when I looked back and saw that…that…dangling participle, the thought that crossed my mind was, I am going to die!

I knew they were my pantyhose because the right foot was securely wrapped around my ankle. I knew it was secure because I tried to shake the thing off and pretend I had picked it up in the street.

It's amazing to me that we gals buy these things in flat little packages, we wear them once, and they grow. Now I had a mammoth handful of panty hose and no place to pitch them. The shelves were crowded with groceries, and my purse was too small and full, so I stuffed them in my coat pocket. They became a protruding hump on my right hip.

I decided to never leave that store. I knew all the store employees in town, and I figured that by now they would have all their employees at the windows waiting for a return parade.

I glanced cautiously around the store and noticed it was Senior Citizens' Day. They were having their blood pressures read, so I got in line to avoid having to leave the store.

The bad news was no one noticed I didn't belong in line. The good news was I had an elevated blood pressure reading. Usually the nurses take mine and say, "I'm sorry but you died two days ago." Today I registered well up the scale.

Finally I realized I'd have to leave. I slipped out the door, down the street, into my car and off for home.

All the way home I said, "I'LL NEVER TELL ANY-ONE I DID THIS!"

I made it home and got out of the car. My husband was in the yard raking.

I screamed, "Do you know what I did?!"

He was so proud to know his wife had gone through town dragging her underwear. I told him I thought we should move—to another state—in the night. He thought that was extreme and suggested instead that for a while I could walk ten feet behind him. After thinking that through, we decided it should be ten feet in front of him so he could check me out.

If you have ever done anything to embarrass yourself, you know that the more you try not to think about it, the more it comes to you in living color. As I walked through my house, the replay of what I did came to me again and again.

At last I cried out to the Lord, "You take ashes and create beauty, but can You do anything with panty hose?"

A Street Vendor Named Contentment

Max Lucado

Ahhh...an hour of contentment. A precious moment of peace. A few minutes of relaxation. Each of us has a setting in which contentment pays a visit.

Early in the morning while the coffee is hot and everyone else is asleep.

Late at night as you kiss your six-year-old's sleepy eyes.

In a boat on a lake when memories of a life well-lived are vivid.

In the companionship of a well-worn, dog-eared, even tearstained Bible.

In the arms of a spouse.

At Thanksgiving dinner or sitting near the Christmas tree.

An hour of contentment. An hour when deadlines are forgotten and strivings have ceased....

But unfortunately, in our squirrel cages of schedules, contests, and side-glancing, hours like these are about as common as one-legged monkeys. In our world, contentment is a strange street vendor, roaming, looking for a home, but seldom finding an open door. This old salesman moves slowly from house to house, tapping on windows, knocking on doors, offering his wares: an hour of peace, a smile of acceptance, a sigh of relief. But his goods are seldom taken. We are too busy to be content....

"Not now, thank you. I've too much to do," we say. "Too many marks to be made, too many achievements to be achieved, too many dollars to be saved, too many promotions to be earned. And besides, if I'm content, someone might think I've lost my ambition."

So the street vendor named Contentment moves on.

***

My list of things was, for the most part, undone. My responsibilities were just as burdensome as ever. Calls to be made. Letters to be written. Checkbooks to be balanced.

But a funny thing happened on the way to the rat race that made me slip into neutral. Just as I got my sleeves rolled up, just as the old engine was starting to purr, just as I was getting up a good head of steam, my infant daughter, Jenna, needed to be held. She had a stomachache. Mom was in the bath so it fell to Daddy to pick her up.

She's three weeks old today. At first I started trying to do things with one hand and hold her with the other. You're smiling. You've tried that too? Just when I realized that it was impossible, I also realized that it was not at all what I was wanting to do.

I sat down and held her tight little tummy against my chest. She began to relax. A big sigh escaped her lungs. Her whimpers became gurgles. She slid down my chest until her little ear was right on top of my heart. That's when her arms went limp and she fell asleep.

And that's when the street vendor knocked at my door.

Good-bye, schedule. See you later, routine. Come back tomorrow, deadlines…hello Contentment, come on in.

Growing Roots

Philip Gulley

Had an old neighbor when I was growing up named Doctor Gibbs. He didn't look like any doctor I'd ever known. Every time I saw him, he was wearing denim overalls and a straw hat whose front brim was green sunglass plastic. He smiled a lot, a smile that matched his hat—old and crinkly and well worn. He never yelled at us for playing in his yard. I remember him as someone who was a lot nicer than circumstances warranted.

When Doctor Gibbs wasn't saving lives, he was planting trees. His house sat on ten acres and his life goal was to make it a forest. The good doctor had some interesting theories concerning plant husbandry. He came from the "No pain, no gain" school of horticulture. He never watered his new trees, which flew in the face of conventional wisdom. Once I asked why. He said watering plants spoiled them, and how if you water them, each successive generation will grow weaker and weaker. So you have to make things rough for them and weed out the weenie trees early on.

He talked about how watering trees made for shallow roots, and how trees that weren't watered had to grow deep roots in search of moisture. I took him to mean that deep roots were to be treasured.

So he never watered his trees. He'd plant an oak and, instead of watering it every morning, he'd beat it with a rolled-up newspaper. Smack! Slap! Pow! I asked him why he did that, and he said it was to get the tree's attention.

Doctor Gibbs went to glory a couple of years after I left home. Every now and again I walk by his house and look at the trees that I watched him plant some twenty-five years ago.

They're granite strong now. Big and robust. Those trees wake up in the morning and beat their chests and drink their coffee black.

I planted a couple of trees a few years back. Carried water to them for a solid summer. Sprayed them. Prayed over them. The whole nine yards. Two years of coddling has resulted in trees that expect to be waited on hand and foot. Whenever a cold wind blows in, they tremble and chatter their branches. Sissy trees.

Funny thing about those trees of Doctor Gibbs. Adversity and deprivation seemed to benefit them in ways comfort and ease never could.

Every night before I go to bed, I check on my two sons. I stand over them and watch their little bodies, the rising and falling of life within. I often pray for them. Mostly I pray that their lives will be easy. "Lord, spare them from hardship." But lately I've been thinking that it's time to change my prayer.

Has to do with the inevitability of cold winds that hit us at the core. I know my children are going to encounter hardship, and my praying they won't is naive. There's always a cold wind blowing somewhere.

So I'm changing my eventide prayer. Because life is tough, whether we want it to be or not. Instead, I'm going to pray that my son's roots grow deep, so they can draw strength from the hidden sources of the Eternal God.

Too many times we pray for ease, but that's a prayer seldom met. What we need to do is pray for roots that grow deep into the Eternal God, so when the rains fall and the winds blow, we won't be swept asunder.

Perspective

Marilyn McAuley

A little girl was visiting her grandmother in the country. One evening they sat and enjoyed the panorama of stars in the heavens—such sparkling brilliance the little girl hadn't seen, living in the city with all the lights. She was in awe of the beauty and said to her grandmother, "If heaven is so beautiful on the wrong side, what must it be like on the right side?"

OPPORTUNITY

*When one door closes, another opens
but we often look so long and so regretfully
upon the closed door
that we do not see the one which
has opened for us.*

Alexander Graham Bell

Saving the Broken Pieces

Robert Schuller

At the Royal Palace of Tehran in Iran, you can see one of the most beautiful mosaic works in the world. The ceilings and walls flash like diamonds in multifaceted reflections.

Originally, when the palace was designed, the architect specified huge sheets of mirrors on the walls. When the first shipment arrived from Paris, they found to their horror that the mirrors were shattered. The contractor threw them in the trash and brought the sad news to the architect.

Amazingly, the architect ordered all of the broken pieces collected, then smashed them into tiny pieces and glued them to the walls to become a mosaic of silvery, shimmering, mirrored bits of glass.

Broken to become beautiful! It's possible to turn your scars into stars. It's possible to be better because of the brokenness. It is extremely rare to find in the great museums of the world objects of antiquity that are unbroken. Indeed, some of the most precious pieces in the world are only fragments that remain a hallowed reminder of a glorious past.

Never underestimate God's power to repair and restore.

Train to Barcelona

Jori Senter Stuart

It was spring break, I was 18 and life was wonderful. I had just completed one semester of school in Germany and was on my way to a second term in England. Between semesters, a friend and I decided to do a little sightseeing and had charted our course to cover eight countries in twenty-eight days.

We had just spent a few days basking in the sun-filled little town of Nice along the French Riviera. Now our francs had almost run out—a sign it was time to pack up and move on. We stuffed our meager belongings into our backpacks and lumbered to the train station like a couple of pack mules.

By the time we arrived at the train station, the mass of humanity waiting for trains had already begun to spill out into the streets. Apparently, all 50,000 college students on spring break were trying to take the morning train out of Nice. As we elbowed our way to the ticket counter, we kept hearing the ominous words: "train strike."

"No trains," the man behind the counter confirmed. "May be a day. May be a week."

Discouraged, we looked for a spot to set up camp. Once settled, we took stock of our situation. Between the two of us, we had enough food to last the day. Bottled water, two peanut butter-jelly sandwiches and two oranges. Our monetary supply consisted of exactly twelve francs. Suddenly we felt a very long way from home.

Seven hours later, the scene had not changed much except the crowd was larger, tempers were hotter, and word of the stranded tourists had made it out to the streets. Rough looking teens began to slouch among the throng, looking for easy targets. I was comforted some by the group of American students who were camped out next to us. They were busy playing cards and writing postcards home.

"I'm going to call around and find a way out of this place." My friend was obviously growing impatient. "You watch the stuff and I'll go make a few phone calls."

I wadded my jacket against the pillar and tried to settle in for the night. Things were growing quieter in the station.

Suddenly, from behind the pillar I heard the voice hissing at me, "Don't say anything. Just give me your money and your passport and we'll leave you alone."

He had come out from behind the pillar and stood tall and menacing in front of me. His hat hung low over his eyes.

"I'm sorry. I don't understand...." I was hoping he would get frustrated and give up.

He obviously was not so easily put off.

"You know what I want, American. I suggest you stop playing games with me before I get really angry...."

Even as he spit the words at me, a stranger from the group of American students next to us had grabbed my arm and was pulling me to my feet.

"Our train has just pulled in. Grab your pack and let's go before we lose our seats."

A blond pony-tailed girl in baggy sweatshirt and jeans was hoisting my friend's backpack onto her shoulders, chatting to me all the while.

"Where did you go? I've been looking all over for you...come on, we have to run. You will excuse us, won't you?" She brushed us both past the would-be robber. He was too surprised to say anything but in one last-ditch effort he grabbed at my arm. My rescuer was too quick for him as she propelled me through the crowd.

After what seemed an eternity of pushing and shoving, we reached a clearing in the crowd. Shaking, I set my backpack beside a bench and turned to thank the one who had just saved me. But all I found was my friend's red backpack, leaning neatly up against the wall. The gray sweatshirt and blond ponytail had disappeared back into the crowd.

Suddenly I heard my name being called.

"Jori." My friend was running down the platform toward me. "Where have you been? Why didn't you stay by the pillar?"

We sat down on the bench and I began to tell my adventure. I was interrupted by the announcement over the public address system.

"Train to Barcelona now arriving on Track 4. Train to Barcelona now arriving on Track 4."

We looked up at the platform number above our heads and saw we were sitting on platform number 4! Already we could see the engine's light shining at us from down the track.

Later, as we watched the French countryside glide by outside our train window, I said to my friend, "And I didn't even get to say thank you to her."

My friend said simply, "I think she knows."

And somehow, I felt she did too.

*For he will command his angels concerning you to
guard you in all your ways.*

PSALM 91:11

Sandcastles

Max Lucado

Hot sun. Salty air. Rhythmic waves. A little boy is on the beach. On his knees he scoops and packs the sand with plastic shovels into a bright red bucket. Then he upends the bucket on the surface and lifts it. And, to the delight of the little architect, a castle tower is created.

All afternoon he will work. Spooning out the moat. Packing the walls. Bottle tops will be sentries. Popsicle sticks will be bridges. A sandcastle will be built.

Big city. Busy streets. Rumbling traffic.

A man is in his office. At his desk he shuffles papers into stacks and delegates assignments. He cradles the phone on his shoulder and punches the keyboard with his fingers. Numbers are juggled and contracts are signed and much to the delight of the man, a profit is made.

All his life he will work. Formulating the plans. Forecasting the future. Annuities will be sentries. Capital gains will be bridges. An empire will be built.

Two builders of two castles. They have much in common. They shape granules into grandeurs. They see nothing and make something. They are diligent and determined. And for both the tide will rise and the end will come.

Yet that is where the similarities cease. For the boy sees the end while the man ignores it. Watch the boy as the dusk approaches.

As the waves near, the wise child jumps to his feet and begins to clap. There is no sorrow. No fear. No regret. He knew this would happen. He is not surprised. And when the great breaker crashes into his castle and his masterpiece is sucked into the sea, he smiles. He smiles, picks up his tools, takes his father's hand, and goes home.

The grownup, however, is not so wise. As the wave of years collapses on his castle he is terrified. He hovers over the sandy monument to protect it. He blocks the waves from the walls he has made. Salt-water soaked and shivering he snarls at the incoming tide.

"It's my castle," he defies.

The ocean need not respond. Both know to whom the sand belongs....

And I don't know much about sandcastles. But children do. Watch them and learn. Go ahead and build, but build with a child's heart. When the sun sets and the tides take—applaud. Salute the process of life, take your Father's hand, and go home.

Every man is entitled to be valued
by his best moments.

Ralph Waldo Emerson

The Crazy Quilt

Melody Carlson

I have an old quilt made by my father's grandmother. It's not a beautiful quilt, and all the fabric appears to be quite old. But I love it.

The pieces are probably left over scraps from Aunt Fran's apron, little Mary's Easter dress, or Grampa's favorite shirt. They are odd shapes and sizes. Some nameless shapes have hooks and curves, long slivers of fabric painstakingly sewn with dozens of meticulous stitches. A few tiny patches are smaller than my thumbnail.

Some of the fabric is very plain with dull color. I can just hear some tired mother say, "But, dear, it's a very serviceable cloth…," while her daughter frowns at the new school dress. Other pieces are bright and cheery, like snippets of birthdays, summer vacations, and fun times gone by. A few fancier pieces are satiny smooth with embossing or embroidery; they seem to whisper of weddings, dances, a first kiss.…

My father's grandmother was nearly blind and perhaps that explains why the shades appear haphazardly arranged and almost seem to shout at each other. I wonder if she ever realized what her creations looked like, or did she simply go by touch? They do have an interesting texture—smooth next to bumpy, seersucker alongside velvet; and all over the quilt hundreds of tiny stitches, almost invisible to the eye, pucker ever so slightly.

If I were blind, I would like to make quilts like this.

Recently my own family relocated to a new town, and I was in bed with the flu, wrapped in my great grandmother's crazy quilt. I felt sorry for myself and I missed the friends I'd left behind. Deep down, I knew it was partly my own fault—I hadn't taken steps to establish new friendships. Several acquaintances seemed willing, but I was holding back, hesitating....

As I studied the crazy quilt, I thought of the many friends I'd had throughout my life. Some felt a bit scratchy and rough like a sturdy piece of wool, but in time they softened—or I became used to them. Others were delicate like silk and needed to be handled with care. Some were colorful and bright and great fun to be with. A few special others felt soft and cozy like flannel, and they knew how to make me feel better.

Many of my friends have only been around for a season. So often I've had to leave them behind, or they leave me! And yet, in my heart, I know they are friends for life. If I met them on the street tomorrow, we would hug and laugh and talk nonstop. It would seem like yesterday.

And that's because God has sewn them into my heart.

I pulled the old quilt closer around me, comforted and warmed by my memories. Surely, my own masterpiece—this quilt of friendships I fretted over—was not nearly finished, I would make new friends in this town. And like my great grandmother, trusting her fingers to lead her, I would, by faith, reach out.

One Man's Junk...
Another Man's Treasure

Ron Mehl

B ob had systematically worked his way to the back of the garage and was about to make his exit when he first saw it.

Although partially hidden underneath a table cloth and an old comforter, the shape was unmistakable. It was a motorcycle. And not only that...it was a Harley.

Obviously it wasn't part of the garage sale, and that piqued Bob's interest.

"Is the bike for sale?"

The man shrugged. "Well...I don't rightly see why not. The wife says it's all got to go. But I'll warn ya. That bike hasn't run since I've had it. Motor's seized up. Won't turn over. Could probably buy yourself a new one with what it'd cost to fix up that old thing."

Bob nodded patiently. "All the same, how much do you want for it?"

"I'm sure they'd give me thirty-five bucks for the metal at the scrap yard. How does that sound?"

Bob looked at the rusty old heap. What would his wife say if he brought it home? But still...to a practiced eye, it had potential. Even if it didn't run, he could get it shined up as a conversation piece. And he could surely sell it again for more than thirty-five dollars. Parts alone would be worth more than that.

"Okay," he said. "I'll give you thirty-five. Can I pick it up tomorrow?"

Shortly thereafter the old Harley was occupying space in Bob's garage. After a few weeks of procrastinating, he finally got around to calling Harley-Davidson, just to see what a few major parts for restoration would run him. He connected with someone on the parts line and asked a few questions.

"Why don't you give me the serial number," the dealer said, "and I can look that up for you."

Bob gave him the number.

"Hold on just a second while I look it up."

Bob waited on hold, listening to a sixties rock station piped into the receiver. *How appropriate,* he thought. After what seemed an inordinately long time, the parts man returned to the line. And just in time. One more number by the Trogs or Country Joe and the Fish might have driven Bob off the line altogether.

Somehow the Harley man sounded different. Strange. Self-conscious. Like something was up.

"Uh, sir…I'm going to have to call you back, okay? Could I get your full name, address, and phone number, please?"

Why does he need my name and address? Bob wondered. But then again, what was the harm? It was no big deal. He'd probably end up on some motorcycle list. Bob gave the man what he wanted and hung up.

After a few minutes, however, he found himself getting nervous. He regretted giving the information about himself over the phone. *What if the bike had been involved in a crime of some kind…? What if the bike was stolen? Was he in danger of prosecution? Maybe the police were already on their way—or a Hell's Angel, ready to reclaim his bike….*

Bob sweated for a couple of days without hearing back from Harley. But just as his worries were beginning to subside, the phone rang. This time, however, it wasn't the parts man; Bob found himself talking to a Harley executive. The man seemed overly friendly, making Bob feel even more uneasy.

"Listen, Bob," said the man, "I want you to do something for me, okay?"

"Umm. Well, I guess."

"Bob, I want you just to set the receiver down—don't hang up—and take the seat off your bike and see if anything is written underneath. Would you do that for me, Bob?" The man talked like an air traffic controller bringing in an off-course 737.

And Bob felt like he was about to hit wind shear.

But he grabbed a screwdriver, did as he was told, and returned to the phone. "Yes," he said, "it does have something written there. It's engraved, and it says, 'THE KING.' Listen, is there some kind of trouble here? What's this all about?"

There was a moment or two of profound silence on the other end. Bob felt like the man on the long distance commercial listening for a pin to drop.

"Bob, my boss has authorized me to offer you $300,000 for the bike, payable to you immediately. How about it? Do we have a deal?"

Bob was so stunned he could hardly speak. "I-I'll have to think about it," he stammered. He hung up the phone and let himself slump slowly to a sitting position on the kitchen floor.

The next day Bob got a call from Jay Leno, the late-night television talk sultan. Leno explained that he "had a thing about Harleys" and offered Bob $500,000.

"The King," of course, was none other than Elvis Presley. The serial number had made that clear, and the engraved legend under the seat had removed all doubt. The bike Bob had redeemed from the scrap pile for thirty-five dollars had once been owned by "The King of Rock 'n Roll." And it was worth half a million—*at the least.* After all those years of seeking "The Big Find," Bob found it. But he hadn't even recognized what he had.

It goes to show you that truly one man's junk is another man's treasure. The value of the motorcycle, of course, wasn't in the metal or the parts. It didn't even run! The value had nothing to do with the bike's beauty, what it was made of, or how well it performed.... It was all tied to the fact that it had been owned by "the King." He had touched it, ridden it, taken pride in it. And the inexplicable value our culture has attached to Elvis Presley—approaching deity status—transferred to his motorcycle. There were people willing to pay a small fortune for the privilege of saying, "I own Elvis Presley's motorcycle."

Bob didn't realize he had something of great value. He hadn't a clue about the bike's previous owner. He just saw something cheap on the marketplace—an opportunity for a little profit. What he found out, of course, was that ownership was by far the most important truth about that old Harley. In fact, ownership was *everything*.

And what is it that speaks most forcefully about your value and mine?

Is it what we're made of? Is it based on our job title or economic status? Is it determined by what we can do and how we "perform"? ...What gives me a sense of worth and significance is that I belong to God. I have been redeemed by God's own Son at great suffering and a great price. He owns me....No one argues with the mark of the King.

Commence Prayer

Charles Swindoll

The plane was headed for New York—a routine and normally very boring flight. But this time it proved to be otherwise.

As they were on their descent pattern, the pilot realized that the landing gear was not engaging. He messed around with the controls, trying again and again to get the gear to lock into place...without success. He then asked ground control for instruction. As the plane circled the landing field, the emergency crew coated the runway with foam and fire trucks and other emergency vehicles moved into position.

Meanwhile, the passengers were told of each maneuver in that calm, unemotional voice pilots do so well. Flight attendants glided about the cabin with an air of cool reserve. Passengers were told to place their heads between their knees and grab their ankles just before impact. There were tears and a few cries of despair....

Then, with the landing only minutes away, the pilot suddenly announced over the intercom: "We are beginning our final descent. At this moment, in accordance with International Aviation Codes established at Geneva, it is my obligation to inform you that if you believe in God you should commence prayer." Scout's honor...that's exactly what he said!

Secret Cracks and Crevices

Melody Carlson

Grandma's tall Victorian house looked like a castle to me as a child. Proud and white, it roosted on a grassy knoll skirted by a colorful flower bed. Total strangers would pause to admire and even photograph Grandma's striking rock garden. But the three-hour trip to Grandma's house amounted to more than merely visiting her turreted home with its gingerbread trim and pretty flowers; it meant entering a world unlike my everyday one.

At Grandma's, everything changed, and I encountered a secret world—a world where only I knew all the fascinating nooks and crannies. I could dawdle away countless summer hours exploring its hidden corners. I remember the warm, earthy smell after a summer shower and the feel of the cool, damp cement through my thin cotton shorts as I sat on the steps behind Grandma's house. Lush, leafy fuchsia plants profuse with luxuriant purplish flowers overflowed the deep beds that bordered those steps. They looked like miniature Japanese lanterns, and the honeybees scurried about them gathering food. I remember the waxen feel of an unopened fuchsia blossom and the pop it made when pinched gently by my fingers— and the muffled, angry buzz of the unfortunate bee I imprisoned in the royal-colored depths of a bloom.

I would climb up those fuchsia-bordered steps to the home of Martha—Grandma's neighbor. Her flagstone patio, still wet from the rain, steamed and glistened in the afternoon sun. Beside her patio grew a small garden surrounded by a child-sized fence. I'd stand and lean my arms upon it and inspect the mysterious green foliage flourishing within. A clothesline stretched high over the garden. On one end hung a pulley my grandpa had designed to draw the flapping whites to and fro without having to set foot in Martha's garden. Martha and Grandma shared the line, dividing the sunshine between them.

Inside her sun-filled front room, Martha kept building blocks and wooden dolls, picture books and an old 3-D photo viewer—all for her young visitors. Of course, cookies and tea would invariably be served; it was a little girl's utopia.

Down the street lived Grandma's sister, Londy. Londy's house reminded me of Snow White's cottage. Surrounded by towering trees and tucked in so neatly, it might have sprouted like an oversized mushroom. Londy, a tiny woman, fit flawlessly with her diminutive house. She liked to bustle about and prepare delectable snacks in her compact kitchen. She'd array toast and homemade preserves on flowery china for her much-welcomed guests, and she never discriminated between children and adults—we all ate from the same dainty dishes; no plastic was found in her kitchen.

Londy enjoyed cut flowers, and they often cascaded from the porcelain vases in her home. Outside her kitchen window grew roses, berry bushes, and mint. The mixture of their fragrances was almost intoxicating as it wafted in on a warm summer breeze. Londy's home felt like an enchanted, full-grown dollhouse.

At Grandma's house, I'd be the first one up in the morning because I knew Grandpa had breakfast sizzling and steaming downstairs in the cozy kitchen. After eating, I'd linger at the table in front of the big picture window, where the bright red geraniums bloomed year round in the window box. I'd try to spy the little green frog who lived in the geraniums and watch the hummingbirds flitter about the hanging flower baskets. Summers were timeless then—no schedule, no routine.

Although the places remain, the people are gone; and I'm torn between the desire to return and discover what time has done to my childhood paradise and the fear that the spell, now broken, would only bring disappointment. For the places I remember, even if they have remained unchanged, can never be found again because my child's eye perceived the hill as a mountain and the house as a castle. And so these memories must continue to endure in the secret places—hidden in the cracks and crevices—only to be visited through remembering.

MAKE A PEARL

The most extraordinary thing about the oyster is this: irritations get into his shell. He does not like them. But when he cannot get rid of them, he uses the irritation to do the loveliest thing an oyster ever has a chance to do. If there are irritations in our lives today, there is only one prescription: make a pearl.

Harry Emerson Fosdick

Back on Course

Sandy Snavely

My husband and I love to sail. We named our 27-foot sailboat the *Sensuous Sea* because it represents for us how seductive the water can be to our sense of adventure. When the water is calm and the wind is stable, sailing is a profoundly rich experience. Yet there are times when the water turns evil and the wind breathes terror through our veins like an invisible enemy.

One day, while heading up the Columbia River on our way to Astoria, a sea condition appropriately known as "widow makers" interrupted our peaceful voyage. Five to six-foot waves slammed against us, one right after the other, and we steadied ourselves for a bumpy ride.

Suddenly, Bud heard a sound that appeared to be coming from the bow. Straining to see forward through the water that the wind whipped around us, he discovered that our anchor had become dislodged from the pulpit. It was banging against our hull. With each thud, the danger of beating a hole into the fiberglass increased, threatening our safety.

Bud then did the most frightening thing I've ever seen him do. With neither a life jacket nor a life line, he made his way forward to the point of the bow, leaving me in the cockpit to man the tiller as he retrieved the anchor.

One of my strong-suits in sailing has always been my ability to keep our boat on course—until that moment when my husband's life was hanging precariously over the edge of the boat. Wave after angry wave crashed over him, like great sea gypsies trying to snatch him away from me. Steadying my focus on Bud, I immediately began to plan what I would do to rescue him if indeed he went overboard.

The sound of my husband's voice shouting to me through the storm broke the hold fear had on me and snapped me back to reason: "Get back on course! Point her toward the marker!"

Prying my focus off of my husband and setting my sights back to the marker was the most difficult order I have ever been called to obey. It was against all my instincts to turn my back on what seemed to be the need of the moment, and trust the rules of the water. As I heeded Bud's command, however, I was able to get us back on course. Bud fastened the anchor into its holder and we were once again headed in the right direction.

We both learned a valuable lesson that afternoon: danger lurks around every corner, and we can be distracted from our real goals, tempted to change the rules to solve what seems to be life's more immediate crises.

But there are sound principles designed to bring us safely to our destination if we are willing to trust them and not be swayed off course by sudden fears. We must be determined to study the charts, follow the rules, and steady the course or we will end up over our heads in deep water when life's storms hit.

YOUNG OR OLD?

An elderly lady was asked by a child if she were young or old.

"My dear," she replied. "I have been young a very long time."

from P.S. I Love You

Redwood Canyon

Casandra Lindell

My grandpa smelled of old leather, fresh dirt, and clean stale sweat. He wore short-sleeved denim shirts, blue jeans held by red suspenders, and the green aftershave by Mennen. When I was very little, his hat of choice was what my brother and I called his "safari hat"—a round gray helmet made of hard plastic with a brim all the way around and molded seams.

Grandpa never really got past the idea that horses were essential to life, and he put me on them from as early as I can remember. Being on horseback still makes me feel important and special; being with Grandpa did that. I think he always knew that he'd take me to Redwood Canyon and show me how much of his heart was there. When he and Grandma were first married, they spent summers deep in the Sierras.

I remember the sound of hoofs stamping metal as we backed the horses out of the trailer for that very first ride in Redwood Canyon. The smell of leather and horse manure as we saddled them, Ben snorting and puffing in anticipation, dancing in the dust.

As we rode, Grandpa pointed out wild strawberries lining the path; I had no idea they were so tiny. I would have missed them.

Grandpa knew the difference between the sound of far-off water trickling and wind in the trees, but I didn't. Once, I guessed it was wind. Grandpa smiled: "Nope. Follow me." He veered downhill, off the trail. I followed, a little unsure of myself.

He came to a stop, pushing back the brim of his cowboy hat. I pulled Ben up alongside and followed Grandpa's eyes.

To this day I have never seen a more peaceful place. Below us a stream meandered through fern and wild tiger lilies to silently drop ten feet into a small crystal pool. Beside the pool was a sandy beach and a fallen log. I thought of Eden undisturbed. We sat long enough for that image to sink forever into my soul. I still close my eyes and look at that crystal pool when I need a few moments of peace.

Further along the trail, a clearing in the trees caused a faraway smile to tug the corners of Grandpa's mouth. In front of us lay a beach of fist-sized rocks. A stream, trying to go unnoticed, spread out to pick its way through the rocks before regrouping once past the clearing.

"We set up camp, our tent right there. Your grandma strung the clothesline between those two trees.... Shot a deer right up over that ridge." Grandpa brought a past and forgotten world to life for me.

"There's an underground stream, runs right along there," Grandpa said, pointing again.

"How do you know that?"

"A straight line of saplings. Seeds that drop will grow where there is water."

Then, as the trail wrapped around the mountain, we came face to face with a tree laying across our path. This was Redwood Canyon. Giant redwoods. The fallen tree was at least fifteen feet in diameter—which meant a fifteen-foot wall of redwood towering above us. Downhill, tangled limbs. Uphill, a gaping hole in the earth and a massive root system.

My face fell. We'd have to turn back. Grandpa simply sat and looked at the tree. I looked at Grandpa.

"We have to go back now?" I asked, disappointed.

He sat still and looked at the fallen tree. Then, with a glance, Grandpa whirled his horse, kicked his heels, and called over his shoulder, "Come on!"

I watched, his horse slipping in the fallen leaves and needles as they climbed. No way was I going up that mountain. I'd fall. The horse'd fall. We'd *both* fall.

But the problem was that I knew my grandpa—he would wait all day at the top if he had to, until I followed him. He was known for tenacity. Grandpa never really got over the idea that the best way to learn was to tackle the impossible.

"Come on!" I heard Grandpa's voice call to me again. "Let the horse find his own way. He doesn't want to fall any more than you do."

I knew I could trust my Grandpa in the Sierras. He had, after all, spent a lifetime on horseback, and he knew the mountains well.

So I did the only thing I could: I grabbed the saddle horn, loosened the reins—and shut my eyes tight as I kicked my heels.

Ben jumped forward, scrambling up the mountain. It was a bumpy ride. After several seconds, I felt him smooth out and I opened my eyes. There sat Grandpa, amusement twinkling all over his rugged face. "You had your eyes closed? You missed the best part of the ride!"

There were so many things I learned that day, and on later rides through Redwood Canyon. More often than anything I see the image of that huge fallen redwood. Life is like that. It would be great if it were all wild strawberries and silent crystal pools. But so many times we come to a place where something big has fallen across the trail. It looms, and we reach a dark impasse.

Then I remember the choice my grandpa taught me. I can give up and go back sadly defeated—or I can hang on, loosen the reins, and follow the One who knows His way around any obstacle. That's what faith is.

And, if we keep our eyes open? We won't miss the best parts.

Life Begins at 80

Author Unknown

I have good news for you. The first 80 years are the hardest. The second 80 are a succession of birthday parties.

Once you reach 80, everyone wants to carry your baggage and help you up the steps. If you forget your name or somebody else's name, or an appointment, or your own telephone number, or promise to be three places at the same time, or can't remember how many grandchildren you have, you need only explain that you are 80.

Being 80 is a lot better than being 70. At 70 people are mad at you for everything. At 80 you have the perfect excuse no matter what you do. If you act foolishly, it's your second childhood. Everybody is looking for symptoms of softening of the brain.

Being 70 is no fun at all. At that age they expect you to retire to a house in Florida and complain about your arthritis (they used to call it lumbago), and you ask everybody to stop mumbling because you can't understand them. (Actually your hearing is about 50 percent gone.)

If you survive until you are 80, everybody is surprised that you are still alive. They treat you with respect just for having lived so long. Actually they seem surprised that you can walk and talk sensibly.

So please, folks, try to make it to 80. It's the best time of life. People forgive you for anything. If you ask me, life begins at 80.

Bus Stop

Patsy Clairmont

Jason, our youngest, has two goals in life. One is to have fun, and the other is to rest. He does both quite well. So I shouldn't have been surprised by what happened when I sent him to school one fall day.

As Jason headed off for the bus, I immediately busied myself, preparing for a full day. The knock on the door was a surprise and disruptive to my morning rhythm, which is not something I have a lot of. I flew to the door, jerked it open, only to find myself looking at Jason.

"What are you doing here?" I demanded.

"I've quit school," He boldly announced.

"Quit school?" I repeated in disbelief and at a decibel too high for human ears.

Swallowing once, I tried to remember some motherly psychology. But all that came to my mind was "A stitch in time saves nine" and "Starve a fever, feed a cold," or something like that. Somehow they didn't seem to apply to a six-year-old dropout dilemma. So I questioned, "Why have you quit school?"

Without hesitation he proclaimed, "It's too long, it's too hard, and it's too boring!"

"Jason," I instantly retorted, "you have just described life. Get on the bus!"

Faith

SEEING GOD

A young man was desperately seeking God. He sought out a wise old man who lived in a nearby beach house and posed the question: "Old man, how can I see God?" The old man who obviously knew God at a depth few of us experience, pondered the question for a very long time. At last he responded quietly: "Young man, I am not sure that I can help you—for you see, I have a very different problem. I cannot not see him."

Author Unknown

Cinderella

Max Lucado

I received a call from a friend named Kenny. He and his family had just returned from Disney World. "I saw a sight I'll never forget," he said. "I want you to know about it."

He and his family were inside Cinderella's castle. It was packed with kids and parents. Suddenly all the children rushed to one side. Had it been a boat, the castle would have tipped over. Cinderella had entered.

Cinderella. The pristine princess. Kenny said she was perfectly typecast. A gorgeous young girl with each hair in place, flawless skin, and a beaming smile. She stood waist-deep in a garden of kids, each wanting to touch and be touched.

For some reason Kenny turned and looked toward the other side of the castle. It was now vacant except for a boy maybe seven or eight years old. His age was hard to determine because of the disfigurement of his body. Dwarfed in height, face deformed, he stood watching quietly and wistfully, holding the hand of an older brother.

Don't you know what he wanted? He wanted to be with the children. He longed to be in the middle of the kids reaching for Cinderella, calling her name. But can't you feel his fear; fear of yet another rejection? Fear of being taunted again, mocked again?

Don't you wish Cinderella would go to him? Guess what? She did!

She noticed the little boy. She immediately began walking in his direction. Politely but firmly inching through the crowd of children, she finally broke free. She walked quickly across the floor, knelt at eye level with the stunned little boy, and placed a kiss on his face.

"I thought you would appreciate the story," Kenny told me. I did. It reminded me of another one. The names are different, but isn't the story almost the same? Rather than a princess of Disney, it's the Prince of Peace. Rather than a boy in a castle, it's a thief on a cross. In both cases a gift was given. In both cases love was shared. In both cases the lovely one performed a gesture beyond words.

But Jesus did more than Cinderella. Oh, so much more.

Cinderella gave only a kiss. When she stood to leave, she took her beauty with her. The boy was still deformed. What if Cinderella had done what Jesus did? What if she assumed his state? What if she had somehow given him her beauty and taken on his disfigurement?

That's what Jesus did.

"He took our suffering on him and felt our pain for us.... He was wounded for the wrong we did; he was crushed for the evil we did. The punishment, which made us well, was given to him, and we are healed because of his wounds."

Make no mistake:

Jesus gave more than a kiss—he gave his beauty.

He paid more than a visit—he paid for our mistakes.

He took more than a minute—he took away our sin.

A New Perspective

Billy Graham

I have a friend who during the Depression lost his job, a fortune, a wife, and a home. But he tenaciously held to his faith—the only thing he had left. One day he stopped to watch some men doing stonework on a huge church. One of them was chiseling a triangular piece of stone. "What are you going to do with that?" asked my friend. The workman said, "See that little opening away up there near the spire? Well, I'm shaping this down here, so it will fit in up there."

Tears filled the eyes of my friend as he walked away, for it seemed that God had spoken through the workman to explain his ordeal through which he was passing, "I'm shaping you down here, so you'll fit in up there."

Treasures in Heaven

Bob Welch

When our pastor spoke recently from the book of Matthew about "not storing up for yourselves treasures on earth, where moth and rust destroy," I couldn't help but think back to an auction I'd once attended.

It was no ordinary auction. The public could bid on unclaimed items that people had left behind in safe-deposit boxes. These items were once deemed so important that people paid money to have them safeguarded in steel.

Diplomas, children's report cards, letters....

I remember how we shuffled along, past the coin collections and pocket watches and jewelry to documents and small items sealed in plastic bags.

Boy Scout patches, receipts from a Waikiki hotel, a child's crayon drawing of a bunny rabbit....

It was all unclaimed property, waiting to be auctioned, the forgotten or overlooked possessions of owners now dead.

Rosaries, letters, train tickets....

Each bag was a mystery, the clues doing more to arouse curiosity than to provide answers. I read the immigration papers of Udolf Matschiner, who arrived at Ellis Island in 1906. Did he find what he was looking for in America?

Two marbles, three stones, and a belt buckle....

Why these things? Did they represent some special memory, some special person?

Passports, telegrams, newspaper clippings....

A yellowed article from a 1959 Los Angeles newspaper was headlined "Vlahovich's Mother Sobs at Guilty Verdict." A mother's son had been convicted of murder. The mother wept, pleading with the judge to spare her son. "Take my blood," she screamed. "Kill me!" What happened? Did she watch her son die in San Quentin's electric chair?

Undeveloped film, birth certificates, marriage certificates....

The official business of life intermingled with the unofficial business of life—a lock of blonde hair, a child's math paper and a poem called "Grandmother's Attic," typed on a typewriter with a sticky e.

> *While up in Grandmother's attic today*
> *In an old red trunk neatly folded away*
> *Was a billowy dress of soft and gray*
> *Of rose brocade were the panniers wide*
> *With quilted patterns down the side*
> *And way in the back against the wall*
> *Of the little old trunk was an old silk shawl*
> *Silver slippers, a fan from France*
> *An invitation to a dance*
> *Written across the program blue*
> *Was "Agatha dear, may I dance with you?"*

It was as if those of us at the auction had been allowed entry into hundreds of Grandmothers' attics, the attics of unknown people.

Diaries, photographs, the ink print of a newborn's feet....

In death's wake, most of the items spoke volumes about life. They also suggested a sense of finality, a realization that life on earth ends, and you can't take anything with you.

So what will we leave behind?

A 6-by-12 box full of mementos can speak volumes about what we valued. But it's only a whisper compared to the legacy of our lives themselves.

Amid our he-who-dies-with-the-most-toys-wins world, perhaps we should dare to leave....

An investment in what God so dearly loves—other people.

An example of a life guided not by the capricious winds of culture, but the rock-solid promises of Christ.

And an inspiration to our children to become all God has designed them to be.

"Store up for yourselves treasures in heaven, where moth and rust do not destroy, and where thieves do not break in and steal," our pastor concluded that Sunday morning. "For where your treasure is, there your heart will be also."

Ah, heaven. The ultimate safe-deposit box.

Hide and Seek

Brother David Steindl-Rast
Retold by Brennan Manning

One day Rabbi Barukh's grandson Yehiel was playing hide-and-seek with another boy. He hid himself well and waited for his playmate to find him. After twenty minutes, he peeked out of his secret hiding place, saw no one, and pulled his head back inside. After waiting a very long time, he came out of his hiding place, but the other boy was nowhere to be seen. Then Yehiel realized that his playmate had not looked for him from the very beginning. Crying, he ran to his grandfather and complained of his faithless friend. Tears brimmed in Rabbi Barukh's eyes as he realized, *God says the same thing: "No one wants to seek me."*

The Lamplighter

Marilyn McAuley

As a young man, the lamplighter led a tough, wayward life. Some years after becoming a Christian, a former friend taunted him about his new lifestyle. The lamplighter finally said, "The only way I can explain it is this: as I go down the street snuffing out the lamps, and I turn around, I see that it's all dark. That is how it was before I met Christ. However, when I continue down the street, the lamps before me light my path—that is how it is with Christ."

The man asked, "And how is it when you've snuffed out *all* the lamps?"

The lamplighter replied, "The dawn is coming."

Soft Cries

Ruth Bell Graham

The cat had kittens on the trundle bed in the downstairs guest room.

We didn't think that was such a good idea, so we collected them and placed them on rags in a cardboard box in front of the kitchen fireplace until we could come up with something more suitable.

But the mother cat had a mind of her own. We watched with amusement as she entered the kitchen silently, stood on her back legs, front legs on the box, sniffing for her babies. Then leaping nimbly over the side, she checked them over, picked one up by the back of the neck, leaped out, and quietly returned it to the trundle bed.

This was repeated till all that was left was the runt of the litter.

She did not come back. She may have been exhausted from her efforts, or she may have been busy playing lunch counter to the others.

We waited.

Finally the tiny scrap in the bottom of the box let out more of a squeak than a mew. It was almost a nonsound.

Instantly, soundlessly, the mother cat appeared, bounded in and out of the box, the littlest kitten in her mouth, and carried it back to the guest room.

Three doors, two rooms, and two hallways, and yet she heard.

The Great Dane had her first litter of pups (two, to be exact) under the lilac bush outside the kitchen window.

After second thoughts she picked up the larger one and carried it to the dog house (around two sides of the house), but being irresponsible, she forgot to return for the second.

After a while number-two pup got hungry. It made the sort of sound newborn pups make, and a very weak one at that.

I could hear the mother coming before I saw her. Galloping like a clap of thunder, she skidded to a stop, and gently lifting the little left-behind by the back of its what-was-supposed-to-be-a-neck, she carried it to join the other.

In neither case was it a full-fledged cry....

Nor are our prayers necessarily full-fledged prayers—or even articulated cries for help.

According to the Bible, God responds to our sighs, our tears, our murmurs—even our longings can be interpreted as prayer.

"The Lord is near to all that call upon him;
yea, he can feel breath when no voice can be heard for faintness."

John Trapp

Spiritual Hero

James Dobson

I heard about this man from a docudrama on television that I saw many years ago. The producer had obtained permission from a cancer specialist to place cameras in his clinic. Then with the approval from three patients, two men and a woman, he captured on film the moment each of them learned they were afflicted with a malignancy in its later stages. Their initial shock, disbelief, fear, and anger were recorded in graphic detail. Afterwards, the documentary team followed these three families through the treatment process with its ups and downs, hopes and disappointments, pain and terror.

He was a humble black pastor of a small inner-city Baptist church. He was in his late sixties and had been a minister throughout his adult life. His love for the Lord was so profound that it was reflected in everything he said. When he and his wife were told he only had a few months to live, they revealed no panic. They quietly asked the doctor what it all meant. When he had explained the treatment program and what they could anticipate, they politely thanked him for his concern and departed. The cameras followed this little couple to their old car and eavesdropped as they bowed their heads and recommitted themselves to the Lord.

In the months that followed, the pastor never lost his poise. Nor was he glib about his illness. He knew the Lord was in control, and he refused to be shaken in his faith.

The cameras were present on his final Sunday in his church. He actually preached the sermon that morning and talked openly about his impending death. To the best of my recollection, this is what he said:

"Some of you have asked me if I'm mad at God for this disease that has taken over my body. I'll tell you honestly that I have nothing but love in my heart for my Lord. He didn't do this to me. We live in a sinful world where sickness and death are the curse man has brought on himself. And I'm going to a better place where there will be no more tears, no suffering, and no heartache. So don't feel bad for me.

"Besides," he continued, "our Lord suffered and died for our sins. Why should I not share in his suffering?" Then he began to sing, without accompaniment, in an old, broken voice.

I wept as this gentle man sang of his love for Jesus. He sounded very weak, and his face was drawn from the ravages of the disease. But his comments were as powerful as any I've ever heard. His words that morning were his last from the pulpit, as far as I know. He slipped into eternity a few days later, where he met the Lord he had served for a lifetime. This unnamed pastor and his wife have a prominent place among my spiritual heroes.

Drifting

Tony Evans

The story is told of a little boy who was floating his boat on a pond when the boat drifted away. A man came by, saw the boat drifting out on the pond, and began throwing stones on the far side of the boat. The boy asked, "What are you doing?"

But then something very interesting happened. As the stones hit the water beyond the boat, they created ripples which pushed the boat back toward the boy. Even though the stones disturbed the smooth water, they achieved the desired result.

That's how it is with God sometimes. When we drift away from Him, He throws the disturbing stones out beyond us in order to push us back to the shore of His love.

Only Glimpses

Alice Gray

Laurel knew she was dying. Over the weeks, we often talked about heaven—what it would look like and how it would be to live there. It seemed we always ended up crying and then holding each other tight in gentle hugs of hope.

The hardest part was trying to imagine something we had never seen, something about which we knew only a little.

And then I remembered this story—

The young girl with the blond hair and the deep blue eyes had been blind since birth. When she was twelve, the doctors were able to perform a new type of surgery that, if successful, would give her the gift of sight. The outcome would not be known for several days. After the bandages were removed, her eyes had to be protected from the light. So she sat in darkness, waiting.

The mother spent long hours answering her daughter's questions about what things looked like and what she should expect. They were both so excited about the possibility of being able to see that neither of them slept much. Over and over, even in the darkness, they talked about every lovely thing they could imagine—colors, shapes, beauty of every kind.

Finally the moment came when the young girl's eyes could endure enough light for her to look out the window. She stood there for a long time without saying a word. Outside, the spring day was ideal—bright and warm with fluffy white clouds decorating the blue sky. Lacy blossoms sprinkled to the ground like pink snow as soft breezes stirred the cherry trees. Yellow crocuses proudly lined the brick walkway that wound across the grass.

When the girl turned back to her mother, tears were streaming down her cheeks. "Oh, Mother. Why didn't you tell me it would be so beautiful?"

I shared this story with my friend, tears filling my own eyes: "Laurel, right now we're sitting in the darkness, but before long you will be asking God the same question."

HOPE

*Faith is the bird that feels
the light and sings
while the dawn is still dark.*

Tagore

The Castle of God's Love

Larry Libby
Condensed from a children's book

Many truths about God are TOO BIG for our minds to hold. We can know some of the truth—and it shines in our hands like star-bright jewels. But there is always more and more and more. More than we can ever know.

We can know a little about God's love, but we could never begin to reach our thoughts around something so mighty.

Sometimes it helps me to think about it like this...

Imagine God's love is a huge castle, soaring higher than a thousand white-peaked mountains—linked together—with their tops poking into space. Imagine looking at this castle from far away. There it is...vast and high, gleaming like morning sun on new snow. Its towers reach up and up toward Heaven. Its windows blaze with bright, welcome light.

This castle is *so great* it would take a lifetime just to walk around it.

You'd love to find out everything you could about that beautiful castle. And there is so much to see and taste and know. Its gardens are bigger than your whole state (even if you live in Alaska) and spill over with towering trees and flowering trees and leaping fountains and majestic waterfalls and deep, bubbling springs and a rainbow of singing birds and—well, who knows what else. Its rooms are filled up with wondrous treasure and music and laughter and mysteries and places where you can explore and play and hide and rest.

No one has seen all its rooms and towers.

No one has eaten in all its long, sunny banquet halls.

No one has peered through all its high windows....

Can you know all of it? No. Not in this world. Not even in a trillion years in Heaven.

But you can find a special room in that castle. A room you'll love so very much. And you can get to know that room, look out of your own window, and at the end of the day curl up in a big soft chair and fall asleep.

Every bit of the castle belongs to you and me, but small as we humans are, we can only enjoy and understand just so much at a time. But we have the rest of our lives here on Earth and endless life in Heaven to keep learning and seeing and hearing more and more.

This is the castle of God's love.

See memo in the note section in the back of the book.

A Vision of Forgiveness

Gigi Tchividjian

Have you ever felt the need for forgiveness...or perhaps the need to forgive?

I meet so many people who are paralyzed in their present circumstances because they're chained to something in their past. They are either unable to forgive or to accept the fact that they are truly forgiven.

I once heard [a legend] of a priest in a small midwestern parish who as a young man had committed what he felt was a terrible sin. Although he had asked God's forgiveness, all his life he carried around the burden of this sin. He just could not be sure God had really forgiven him.

One day he was told of an elderly woman in his congregation who sometimes had visions. During these visions, he had heard, she would often have conversations with the Lord. After a while the priest finally got up enough courage to visit this woman.

She invited him in and offered him a cup of tea. Toward the end of his visit, he set his cup down on the table and looked into the old woman's eyes.

"Is it true that sometimes you have visions?" he asked her.

"Yes," she replied.

"Is it also true that—during these visions—you often speak with the Lord?"

"Yes," she said again.

"Well...the next time you have a vision and speak with the Lord, would you ask Him a question for me?"

The woman looked at the priest a little curiously. She had never been asked this before. "Yes, I would be happy to," she answered. "What do you want me to ask Him?"

"Well," the priest began, "would you please ask Him what sin it was that your priest committed as a young man?"

The woman, quite curious now, readily agreed.

A few weeks passed, and the priest again went to visit this woman. After another cup of tea he cautiously, timidly asked, "Have you had any visions lately?"

"Why yes, I have," replied the woman.

"Did you speak with the Lord?"

"Yes."

"Did you ask Him what sin I committed as a young man?"

"Yes," the woman replied, "I did."

The priest, nervous and afraid, hesitated a moment and then asked, "Well, what did the Lord say?"

The woman looked up into the face of her priest and replied gently, "The Lord told me He could not remember."

God not only forgives our sins, He also chooses to *forget* them. The Bible tells us He takes them and buries them in the deepest sea. And then as Corrie ten Boom used to say, "He puts up a sign that says, 'No fishing allowed.'"

A Meeting of the Minds

Kevin Keller

I heard an interesting story on a radio broadcast. While Benjamin Franklin was in Europe, he met with several of his peers—"a meeting of the minds," so to speak. They came together to review various pieces of literature.

Mr. Franklin chose to read a passage that evoked a curious response from the group.

"This story must be published!" the group chorused. "What is its title?"

"This is really only part of a story," Mr. Franklin replied, "from a book that you have often ridiculed."

The group protested, insisting they would not have rejected a story of such impact.

"In fact," Mr. Franklin continued, "the story that has so moved you all is the book of Ruth—from the Bible."

Running for Daddy!

Kay Arthur

When I was a little girl—just a skinny little beanpole with pigtails—I used to run to my daddy for comfort. I was a tomboy who consistently fell out of trees, got into fights, and crashed my bicycle. It seemed like I was forever bloodying those poor, banged-up knees of mine. That's when I would run—with pigtails flying and dirty tears streaming down my face—to my daddy.

"Daddy! Daddy! Daddy!"

And I'm so fortunate, because I had a daddy who held me. Ever since I was a little girl until the day he went to be with the Lord, I was always his little sweetheart. And I would fly into his open arms, and he would gather me up on his lap—dirt, blood, and all—and hold me there. And he would wipe my tears and push back my pigtails and say, "Now Honey, tell Daddy all about it."

Many years later I was hurting again, so very deeply.

But I couldn't run to my daddy.

I was a single mom with two little kids, trying to work and go to school. And it was one of those days when everything seemed to catch up with me—all of the hurt and loneliness and regret and pressure and weariness. I remember driving into the driveway of the little brick home where we were living. I got out of the car and began walking down the little gravel walkway toward the front door.

For some reason, time seemed to stand still for a moment.

To this day I can't tell you what triggered the thought, but suddenly—in my mind's eye—I saw something.

I saw a little girl, running.

I saw a little girl with tears streaming down her face and

banged-up, bloody knees on those skinny little legs. I saw her in need of her daddy. Running for her daddy.

Then suddenly—strangely—I saw her running down a huge, shiny corridor. A vast corridor with gleaming marble walls and beautiful windows spilling heavenly light. And at the end of that marble hallway were massive doors of brilliant gold. Standing before those doors were bright, powerful guards with great spears.

And I knew that the little girl was me, and that I was running toward the very throne room of God, sovereign ruler of the universe. Yet I was the daughter of the King of Kings, so when the guards saw me coming, they swung open those doors and let me run in. There I was, weeping and running into the very presence of God. I heard the cherubim and the seraphim crying out, "Holy, holy, holy, Lord God Almighty! Heaven and earth are full of Thy glory!" Many bowed before the throne, and court was in session, but I just ran and ran and didn't stop....

I could just see myself running up the wide stairs to that glorious throne—two steps at a time—crying "Abba, Father! *Daddy!*"

And I could see Him stopping everything, opening His arms wide and just gathering me to His chest, saying, "There, there, My precious child. Let Me wipe away those tears. Tell your Father all about it."

Real Treasure

Robin Jones Gunn

We went to Open House tonight at the public elementary school. When Rachel's teacher met us, her eyebrows seemed to elevate slightly. She spoke kindly of our first grader but said she had some concerns. She then invited us to look at the artwork; we would see what she meant.

Dozens of brown paper treasure chests were tacked to the bulletin board. Each had a barreled top attached with a brad. On the front was printed, "A Real Treasure Would Be...." We walked over and began opening the lids to find Rachel's treasure and see why it so concerned the teacher.

As we peeked into each chest, we saw TVs and Nintendos, a few genies, heaps of gold coins, and a unicorn. Rachel's chest was in the very bottom corner. We had to stoop to open it. Inside, our daughter had drawn Christ, hanging on a cross with red drops of blood shaped like hearts dripping from his hands. She had completed the sentence, "A Real Treasure Would Be...Jesus."

"Do you see my concern?" the teacher asked, her arms folded across her chest.

"Yes," my husband agreed, "I see what you mean. The J is backwards, isn't it?"

Calm in the Storm

Ron Mehl

A woman caught in a frightening storm in the middle of the Atlantic Ocean had kept all the little children on board from panicking by telling Bible stories. After finally reaching the dock safely, the ship's captain approached the woman, whom he had observed in the midst of the tempest.

"How were you able to maintain your calm when everyone feared the ship would sink in this storm?" the captain asked. As she looked up, he noted the same quiet peace in her eyes that she had maintained throughout the journey.

"I have two daughters," explained the Christian woman. "One of them lives in New York. The other lives in heaven. I knew I would see one or the other of my daughters in a few hours. And it really didn't matter to me which one."

A Parable of God's Perspective

Robin Jones
Retold by Casandra Lindell

Bert looked into time from heaven and saw the atrocities carried out in the human realm. Absolutely aghast, he pointed to one unspeakable scene and asked God about it. "How can you allow it? Look what evil is setting in motion down there!"

"There's no one better than the devil for creating a tragedy like that!" God said.

"But God, that man is one of your people…oh, that poor man!"

"I gave the freedom to choose between good and evil," God said, his face sad. "No matter what they choose, they all live there together. Sometimes, those who choose my way are impacted by those who don't." He slowly shook his head. "It's always painful when that happens."

"But those people right there have no choice," Bert protested. "Evil is being crammed down their throats! That isn't a choice!"

"Now, Bert," God said patiently, "have I ever let pain go unavenged?"

"No…no, but…" Bert cringed from the sight, unable to bear any more.

"Watch!" God put his arm around Bert's hunched shoulders and turned him again. "Look right over there, by the wall."

"That one? He looks nearly dead. Is he praying?"

"Ah, Bert, you should hear his prayers!" Intense love flashed in God's eyes like lightning. "Simple prayers from an aching heart. *This* is triumph over evil. Trusting me—*that* is the choice." God smiled through sparkling tears of love. "Isn't he magnificent?"

Together they stood in silence, and Bert began to see as God did.

"Now watch this, Bert." God spoke softly, never letting his eyes leave the scene. He called for Michael and the archangel appeared.

"Go down and get him, Michael." The tears of divine joy spilled over. "I'll arrange the party."

Never be afraid to trust
an unknown future
to a known God.

Corrie ten Boom

Worship and Worry

Ruth Bell Graham

It was early in the morning in another country. Exhausted as I was, I awoke around three o'clock. The name of someone I loved dearly flashed into my mind. It was like an electric shock.

Instantly I was wide awake. I knew there would be no more sleep for me the rest of the night. So I lay there and prayed for the one who was trying hard to run from God. When it is dark and the imagination runs wild, there are fears only a mother can understand.

Suddenly the Lord said to me, "Quit studying the problems and start studying the promises."

Now, God has never spoken to me audibly, but there is no mistaking when He speaks. So I turned on the light, got out my Bible, and the first verses that came to me were Philippians 4:6–7 (KJV): "Be careful for nothing; but in every thing by prayer and supplication *with thanksgiving* let your requests be made known unto God. And the peace of God, which passeth all understanding, shall keep your hearts and minds through Christ Jesus" [italics mine]....

Suddenly I realized the missing ingredient in my prayers had been "with thanksgiving." So I put down my Bible and spent time worshipping Him for who and what He is. This covers more territory than any one mortal can comprehend. Even contemplating what little we do know dissolves doubts, reinforces faith and restores joy.

I began to thank God for giving me this one I loved so dearly in the first place. I even thanked Him for the difficult spots which taught me so much.

And you know what happened? It was as if someone

turned on the lights in my mind and heart, and the little fears and worries that had been nibbling away in the darkness like mice and cockroaches hurriedly scuttled for cover.

That was when I learned that worship and worry cannot live in the same heart: they are mutually exclusive.

Fear not tomorrow, for God is already there.

Author Unknown

Are All the Children In?

Author Unknown

I think of times as the night draws nigh
Of an old house on the hill,
Of a yard all wide and blossom-starred
Where the children played at will.

And when deep night at last came down,
Hushing the merry din,
Mother would look all around and ask,
"Are all the children in?"

'Tis many and many a year since then,
And the old house on the hill
No longer echoes childish feet
And the yard is still, so still.

But I see it all as the shadows creep,
And tho' many the years have been
Since then, I can hear my mother ask,
"Are all the children in?"

I wonder if, when those shadows fall
On the last short earthly day,
When we say good-bye to the world outside,
All tired of our childish play,

When we meet the Lover of boys and girls
Who died to save them from sin,
Will we hear Him ask as Mother did,
"Are all the children in?"

Making Adjustments

Ron Mehl

An old sea captain named Eleazar Hall lived in Bedford, Massachusetts, during the time of the great sailing ships. He was renowned, legendary, and revered as the most successful of all sea captains of the day. He worked harder, stayed out longer, and lost fewer men while catching more fish than anyone else.

Captain Hall was often asked about his uncanny ability to stay out so long without navigational equipment. He'd once been gone for two years without coming home for a point of reference.

Eleazar simply replied, "Oh, I just go up on the deck and listen to the wind and rigging. I get the drift of the sea, look up at the stars, and then set my course."

Well, times changed in Bedford. The big insurance companies moved in and said they could no longer insure the ships if the captains didn't have a certified and properly trained navigator on board. They were terrified to tell Eleazar. But to their amazement he said, "If I must, I will go and take the navigational courses."

Eleazar graduated high in his class, and having greatly missed the sea, he immediately took off for a long voyage. On the day of his return, the whole town turned out to ask him the question:

"Eleazar, how was it having to navigate with all those charts and equations?"

Eleazar sat back and let out a long, low whistle. "Oh," he replied, "it was simple. Whenever I wanted to know my location, I'd go to my cabin, get out my charts and tables, work the equations and set my course with scientific precision. Then I'd go up on the deck and listen to the wind and rigging, get the drift of the sea, look at the stars, and go back and correct the errors that I had made in computation."

When I heard that, I prayed, *Lord, I want to know You that way. I want to go up on deck, hear Your quiet voice in my heart, consider Your eternal Word, and then go back down below and make adjustments to all those fine, logical, scientific plans I've drawn up in my head.*

The Artist

Author Unknown

When Leonardo da Vinci had painted his immortal "Last Supper," he asked a friend for an evaluation. The friend heaped superlatives on the masterpiece and especially praised the wine cup by the Lord's hand. At that point, Leonardo blotted out the cup. "Nothing," he was said to have answered, "should distract one's attention from the Lord."

HIS EYE IS ON THE SPARROW

Whenever I am tempted,
whenever clouds arise,
when song gives place to sighing,
when hope within me dies,
I draw the closer to Him,
from care he sets me free...
For His eye is on the sparrow,
and I know He watches me.

Anonymous

The Bells Are Ringing

James Dobson

A nurse with whom I worked, Gracie Schaeffler, had taken care of a five-year-old lad during the latter days of his life. He was dying of lung cancer....

This little boy had a Christian mother who loved him and stayed by his side through the long ordeal. She cradled him on her lap and talked softly about the Lord. Instinctively, the woman was preparing her son for the final hours to come. Gracie told me that she entered his room one day as death approached, and she heard this lad talking about hearing bells ringing.

"The bells are ringing, Mommie," he said. "I can hear them."

Gracie thought he was hallucinating because he was already slipping away. She left and returned a few minutes later and again heard him talking about hearing bells ring.

The nurse said to his mother, "I'm sure you know your baby is hearing things that aren't there. He is hallucinating because of the sickness."

The mother pulled her son closer to her chest, smiled and said, "No, Mrs. Schaeffler. He is not hallucinating. I told him when he was frightened—when he couldn't breathe—if he would listen carefully, he could hear the bells of heaven ringing for him. That is what he's been talking about all day."

That precious child died on his mother's lap later that evening, and he was still talking about the bells of heaven when the angels came to take him....

Heaven

Author Unknown

Think of—

Stepping on shore, and finding it Heaven!
Of taking hold of a hand, and finding it God's hand.
Of breathing a new air, and finding it celestial air.
Of feeling invigorated, and finding it immortality.
Of passing from storm to tempest to an unbroken calm.
Of waking up, and finding it Home.

Notes

If you would like to contribute stories for
another edition of
STORIES FOR THE HEART
or
if you would like to schedule Alice Gray
as a speaker for your group,
please write to the following address:

Alice Gray
1160 NE Greenway Drive
Gresham, OR 97030
Fax: 503-666-3349

When sending stories, please give author's name and original
source if previously published. Also, your own name, address,
and phone number. We will not be able to contact everyone
who submits a story, but will notify you if the story you submit
is used. Manuscripts and photocopies cannot be returned.

I hope these stories have touched your heart
and encouraged your soul. If you wish to reprint any of
the stories, please check the following pages and write directly
to the source where the story was first published

The LORD bless you and keep you;
the LORD make his face shine upon you
and be gracious to you;
the LORD turn his face toward you
and give you peace.

Numbers 6:24-26

If you have enjoyed reading
More Stories for the Heart,
I'd like to recommend the following books:

Stories for the Heart
by Alice Gray
(My first collection of stories.)
$10.99

Someday Heaven
by Larry Libby
(Beautifully written and illustrated for children,
but wonderful for adults, too.
My favorite book about heaven.)
$14.99

Front Porch Tales
by Philip Gulley
(Dramatic stories of courage, humor,
faith and unconditional love.)
$11.99

A Tribute to Moms
by Ruth Senter and Jori Senter Stuart
(Fifty well-known Christian women give
tribute to their moms in this lovely keepsake book.)
$10.99

Christmas Stories for the Heart
by Alice Gray
(A new collection of heart-warming Christmas Stories.
Release date: October 1997.)
$8.99

**All of these books are available, or can be ordered,
at your local bookstore.**

More than a thousand books were researched for this collection of stories as well as reviewing hundreds of stories sent by friends and people whom I have never met. Reasonable care has been taken to trace original ownership, and when necessary, obtain permission to reprint. Some stories have been retold when there was no way to trace the story's origin.

If I have overlooked giving proper credit to anyone, please accept my apologies. If you will contact Multnomah Publishers, Inc., Post Office Box 1720, Sisters, Oregon 97759, corrections will be made prior to additional printings.

Notes and acknowledgments are listed by story title in the order they appear in each section of the book. For permission to reprint copyrighted materials, grateful acknowledgment is made to authors, publishers, and agents—and especially to Multnomah Publishers, Inc.

COMPASSION

"I Want That One" by Charles Stanley from *How to Keep Your Kids on Your Team* (Thomas Nelson, Nashville, TN, © 1986). Used by permission.

"He Needed a Son" author unknown, quoted from *Parables, Etc.*, January 1989, 5.

"Significance" by R.C. Sproul from *The Hunger for Significance* (Regal Books, Ventura, CA, © 1983, 1991).

"Information Please" by Paul Villiard. Reprinted with permission from the June 1966 *Reader's Digest*. (Copyright 1966 by the Reader's Digest Association, Inc.).

"Beethoven's Gift" by Philip Yancey from *Helping the Hurting* (Multnomah Publishers, Inc., Sisters, OR, © 1984). Used by permission.

"Are You God?" by Charles Swindoll from *Improving Your Serve* (Word, Inc., Dallas, TX, © 1981).

"Words Must Wait" by Ruth Bell Graham from *Sitting By My Laughing Fire* (Word Books, Publisher, Waco, TX, © 1977 by Ruth Bell Graham). Used by permission. All rights reserved.

ENCOURAGEMENT

"Mr. Roth" author unknown, quoted in *Leadership Journal*, Fall 1990. Used by permission.

"I Don't Believe a Word of It" by Howard Hendricks from *As Iron Sharpens Iron* (Moody Press, Chicago, IL, © 1995).

"A Perfect Pot of Tea" by Roberta Messner, quoted from *Country Victorian*, Fall 1996. Used by permission of the author. "

"Encouraging Words" by Susan Maycinik from *Discipleship Journal*, July/August 1996. Used by permission.

"Three Letters from Teddy" by Elizabeth Silance Ballard. Original source unknown.

"The Comfort of a Cold, Wet Nose" by Barbara Baumgardner from *Meditations for the Widowed* (Gilgal Publications, Sun River, OR, © 1985). Used by permission of author.

"Giving and Receiving" by Billie Davis, quoted from *The Pentecostal Evangel*, March 17, 1996. Used by permission.

"Teacher Dan" by Marilyn McAuley. Used by permission of the author, © 1997.

"The Mender" by Ruth Bell Graham from *Legacy of a Pack Rat* (Thomas Nelson, Inc., Nashville, TN, © 1989). Used by permission.

"Long Range Vision" by Howard Hendricks from an article in *Ministries Today*, Jan/June 1995.

VIRTUE

LOVE

"50 Promises for Marriage" by Steve Stephens, author of *Marriage: Experience the Best.* Used by permission of the author, © 1996.

"The Treasure" by Alice Gray. Used by permission of the author, © 1997.

"That Little China Chip" by Bettie B. Youngs from *Values from the Heartland: Stories of an American Farmgirl* (Health Communications, Inc., Deerfield Beach, Fl, © 1995 Bettie B. youngs. Reprinted with permission from *Reader's Digest,* June 1996.)

"The Dance" by Thelda Bevens, quoted from *A Passage through Grief* by Barbara Baumgardner (Broadman & Holman Publishers, Nashville, TN, © 1997). Used by permission of Thelda Bevens.

"Don't Forget What Really Matters" by Paul Harvey, appearing in *The Pryor Report,* vol. 10, no. 3A. Used by permission of *The Pryor Report.* Adapted from *Paul Harvey's For What It's Worth.*

"The Last 'I Love You'" by Debbi Smoot, from *Moments for Each Other* by Robert Strand (New Leaf Press, Green Forest, AZ, © 1993) as quoted in *The Pastor's Story File,* February 1992.

FAMILY

"When Grown Kids Come to Visit" by Erma Bombeck from *Forever, Erma* © 1996 by the Estate of Erma Bombeck. All rights reserved. Used by permission of Andrews and McMeel, Kansas City, MO.

"Running Away" by Christopher de Vinck. Reprinted by permission of *Daily Guideposts,* 1995 (Guideposts, Carmel, NY, © 1994).

"Why My Wife Bought Handcuffs" by Philip Gulley from *Front Porch Tales* (Multnomah Publishers, Inc., Sisters, OR, © 1997). Used by permission.

"A Mother's Way" by Temple Bailey, original source unknown.

"Tender Intuition" by Robin Jones Gunn from *Mothering by Heart* (Multnomah Publishers, Inc., Sisters, OR, © 1996). Used by permission.

"Slippery Risks" by Heather Harpham Kopp from *I Stole God from Goody Two-Shoes* (Harvest House Publishing, Eugene, OR, © 1994). Used by permission of author.

"Family Vacations and Other Threats to Marriage" by Philip Gulley from *Front Porch Tales* (Multnomah Publishers, Inc., Sisters, OR, © 1997). Used by permission.

"When God Created Fathers" by Erma Bombeck from *Forever, Erma* © 1996 by the Estate of Erma Bombeck. All rights reserved. Used by permission of Andrews and McMeel, Kansas City, MO.

LIFE

"Lookin' Good" by Patsy Clairmont from *God Uses Cracked Pots* by Patsy Clairmont, published by Focus on the Family. Copyright © 1991, Patsy Clairmont. All rights reserved. International copyright secured. Used by permission.

"A Street Vendor Named Contentment" by Max Lucado from *No Wonder They Call Him the Savior* (Multnomah Publishers, Inc., Sisters, OR, © 1986). Used by permission.

"Growing Roots" by Philip Gulley from *Front Porch Tales* (Multnomah Publishers, Inc., Sisters, OR, ©1997). Used by permission.

"Perspective" by Marilyn McAuley. Used by permission of the author, © 1997.

"Saving the Broken Pieces" by Robert H. Schuller from *Tough-Minded Faith for Tender-Hearted People* (Thomas Nelson, Nashville, TN, © 1983).

"Train to Barcelona" by Jori Senter Stuart. Used by permission of the author, © 1997.

"Sandcastles" by Max Lucado from *The Final Week of Jesus* (Multnomah Publishers, Inc., Sisters, OR, © 1994). Used by permission.

"The Crazy Quilt" by Melody Carlson from *Patchwork of Love* by Heather Harpham Kopp (Multnomah Publishers, Inc., Sisters, OR, © 1997). Used by permission.

"One Man's Junk...Another Man's Treasure" by Ron Mehl from *Meeting God at a Dead End* (Multnomah Publishers, Inc., Sisters, OR, © 1996). Used by permission.

"Commence Prayer" by Charles Swindoll from *Finishing Touch* (Word Publishing, Dallas, TX, © 1994).

"Secret Cracks and Crevices" by Melody Carlson condensed from *Ideals Magazine*, Spring 1993. Used by permission of the author. Melody is a freelance writer and can be reached through Multnomah Publishers, Inc., Sisters, OR.

"Back on Course" by Sandy Snavely, Gresham, OR. Used by permission of the author, © 1996.

"Redwood Canyon" by Casandra Lindell. Condensed. Used by permission of the author, © 1997.

"Life Begins at 80" author and original source unknown.

"Bus Stop" by Patsy Clairmont from *God Uses Cracked Pots* by Patsy Clairmont, published by Focus on the Family. Copyright © 1991, Patsy Clairmont. All rights reserved. International copyright secured. Used by permission.

FAITH

"Cinderella" by Max Lucado from *A Gentle Thunder* (Word, Inc., Dallas, TX, © 1995). Used by permission.

"A New Perspective" by Billy Graham from *The Inspirational Writings of Billy Graham* (Word, Inc., Dallas, TX, © 1995).

"Treasures in Heaven" by Bob Welch. Used by permission of the author, features editor of the *Register-Guard*, Eugene, OR.

"Hide and Seek" by Brother David Steindl-Rast, retold by Brennan Manning in *The Signature of Jesus*, from *Gratefulness, the Heart of Prayer* by Brother David Steindl-Rast (Paulist Press, Mahweh, NJ, © 1984). Used by permission.

"The Lamplighter" by Marilyn McAuley. Used by permission of the author.

"Soft Cries" by Ruth Bell Graham from *Legacy of a Pack Rat* (Thomas Nelson, Inc., Nashville, TN, © 1989). Used by permission.

"Spiritual Hero" by Dr. James Dobson from *When God Doesn't Make Sense* (Tyndale House Publishers, Inc., Wheaton, IL, © 1993). Used by permission. All rights reserved.

"Drifting" by Tony Evans, original source unknown.

"Only Glimpses" by Alice Gray. Used by permission of the author, © 1997.

"The Castle of God's Love" by Larry Libby from *Someone Awesome* (Multnomah Publishers, Inc., Sisters, OR, 1995). Used by permission. Memo from Alice: This is a beautifully written and illustrated gift book for children that answers their questions about God. It is one of my favorite books.

"A Vision of Forgiveness" by Gigi Tchividjian from *Currents of the Heart* (Multnomah Publishers, Inc., Sisters, OR, © 1996). Used by permission.

"A Meeting of the Minds" by Kevin Keller. Used by permission of the author, © 1997.

"Running for Daddy!" by Kay Arthur from *To Know Him by Name* (Multnomah Publishers, Inc., Sisters, OR, © 1995). Used by permission.

"Real Treasure" by Robin Jones Gunn from *Mothering by Heart* (Multnomah Publishers, Inc., Sisters, OR, © 1996). Used by permission.

"Calm in the Storm" by Ron Mehl from *Surprise Endings* (Multnomah Publishers, Inc., Sisters, OR, © 1995). Used by permission.

"A Parable of God's Perspective" by Robin Jones, retold by Casandra Lindell from *Where Was God at 9:02 A.M.?* by Robin Jones and Sandy Dengler (Thomas Nelson, Nashville, TN, © 1995). Used by permission of Casandra Lindell, ©1997.

"Worship and Worry" by Ruth Bell Graham from *Prodigals and Those Who Love Them* (Focus on the Family Publishing, Colorado Springs, CO, © 1991). Used by permission of the author.

"Are All the Children In?" author and original source unknown.

"Making Adjustments" by Ron Mehl from *Surprise Endings* (Multnomah Publishers, Inc., Sisters, OR, © 1995). Used by permission.

"The Artist" quoted from *Today in the Word*, April 1988, published by Moody Bible Institute, Chicago, IL.

"The Bells Are Ringing" by Dr. James Dobson from *When God Doesn't Make Sense* (Tyndale House Publishers, Inc., Wheaton, IL, © 1993). Used by permission, all rights reserved.

"Heaven" author and original source unknown.

Steps to Peace with God

God's Purpose:
Peace and Life

loves you and wants you to experience peace and
–abundant and eternal.

The Bible Says . . .

. . . we have peace with God through our Lord
us Christ." Romans 5:1

For God so loved the world that He gave His
y begotten Son, that whoever believes in Him
uld not perish but have everlasting life."
n 3:16

. . . I have come that they may have life,
that they may have it more abundantly."
n 10:10b

Since God planned
for us to have peace
and the abundant life
right now, why are
most people not hav-
ing this experience?

Our Problem:
Separation

created us in His own image to have an abundant
He did not make us as robots to automatically love
obey Him, but gave us a will and a freedom of
ce.

hose to disobey God and go our own willful way.
till make this choice today. This results in separa-
from God.

Our choice results
in separation from
God.

The Bible Says . . .

For all have sinned and fall short of the glory
od." Romans 3:23

For the wages of sin is death, but the gift of
is eternal life in Christ Jesus our Lord."
ans 6:23

People
(Sinful)

God
(Holy)

Our Attempts

Through the ages, individuals have tried in many ways to bridge this gap . . . without success . . .

The Bible Says . . .

"There is a way that seems right to man, but in the end it leads to death." Proverbs 14:12

"But your iniquities have separated you from God; and your sins have hidden His face from you, so that He will not hear." Isaiah 59:2

There is only o[nly]
remedy for this pr[ob-]
lem of separation.

Step 3 God's Remedy: The Cross

Jesus Christ is the only answer to this problem. He died on the Cross and rose from the grave, paying the penalty for our sin and bridging the gap between God and people.

The Bible Says . . .

". . . God is on one side and all the people on the other side, and Christ Jesus, Himself man, is between them to bring them together . . ." 1 Timothy 2:5

"For Christ also has suffered once for sins, the just for the unjust, that He might bring us to God . . ." 1 Peter 3:18a

"But God demonstrates His own love for us in this: While we were still sinners, Christ died for us." Romans 5:8

God has provided
only way . . . we m[ust]
make the choice .

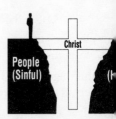

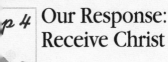

Our Response: Receive Christ

p 4

...ust trust Jesus Christ and receive Him by personal
...tion.

The Bible Says . . .

...ehold, I stand at the door and knock. If
...ne hears My voice and opens the door, I
...ome in to him and dine with him, and he
...Me." Revelation 3:20

...ut as many as received Him, to them He
...the right to become children of God, even
...ose who believe in His name." John 1:12

...if you confess with your mouth the
...Jesus and believe in your heart that God
...aised Him from the dead, you will be saved."
...ns 10:9

Are you here . . . or here?

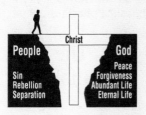

...re any good reason why you cannot receive Jesus Christ right now?

How to receive Christ:

...mit your need (I am a sinner).

...willing to turn from your sins (repent).

...lieve that Jesus Christ died for you on the Cross and rose from the grave.

...rough prayer, invite Jesus Christ to come in and control your life through
...e Holy Spirit. (Receive Him as Lord and Savior.)

What to Pray:

Lord Jesus,
...know that I am a sinner and need Your forgiveness. I believe that You
...for my sins. I want to turn from my sins. I now invite You to come into
...eart and life. I want to trust and follow You as Lord and Savior.

In Jesus' name. Amen.

_____   _____
...te   Signature

God's Assurance: His Word

If you prayed this prayer,

The Bible Says...

"For 'whoever calls upon the name of the Lord will be saved.'" **Romans 10:13**

Did you sincerely ask Jesus Christ to come into your life? Where is He right now? What has He given you?

"For it is by grace you have been saved, through faith—and this is not from yourselves, it is the gift of God—not by works, so that no one can boast." **Ephesians 2:8,9**

The Bible Says...

"He who has the Son has life; he who does not have the Son of God does not have life. These things I have written to you who believe in the name of the Son of God, that you may know that you have eternal life, and that you may continue to believe in the name of the Son of God." **1 John 5:12–13, NKJV**

Receiving Christ, we are born into God's family through the supernatural work of the Holy Spirit who indwells every believer...this is called regeneration or the "new birth."

This is just the beginning of a wonderful new life in Christ. To deepen this relationship you should:

1. Read your Bible every day to know Christ better.
2. Talk to God in prayer every day.
3. Tell others about Christ.
4. Worship, fellowship, and serve with other Christians in a church where Christ is preached.
5. As Christ's representative in a needy world, demonstrate your new life by your love and concern for others.

God bless you as you do.

Billy Graham

If you want further help in the decision you have made, write to:
Billy Graham Evangelistic Association P.O. Box 779, Minneapolis, Minnesota 55440-0779